# PRICE TO PROFIT

P2P

AF582986

# PRICE TO PROFIT

P2P

*Authored by*

SHAILENDRA MARATHE

Office No. 303, Kumar House Building,
D Block, Central Market, Opp PVR Cinema,
Prashant Vihar, Delhi 110085, India
Website: www.penmanbooks.com
Email: publish@penmanbooks.com

First Published by Penman Books 2020
Copyright © Shailendra Marathe 2020
All Rights Reserved.

Title: Price to Profit - P2P
Price: ₹599 | $15
ISBN: 978-93-89024-61-6

No part of this book may be reproduced or transmitted in any form whatsoever, electronic, or mechanical, including photocopying recording, or by any informational storage or retrieval system without the expressed written, dated and signed permission from the author.

LIMITS OF LIABILITY/DISCLAIMER OF WARRANTY: The author and publisher of this book have used their best efforts in preparing this material. The author and publisher make no representation or warranties with respect to the accuracy, applicability or completeness of the contents. They disclaim any warranties (expressed or implied), or merchantability for any particular purpose. The author and publisher shall in no event be held liable for any loss or other damages, including but not limited to special, incidental, consequential, or other damages. The information presented in this publication is compiled from sources believed to be accurate, however, both the publisher and author assume no responsibility for errors or omissions. The information in this publication is not intended to replace or substitute professional advice. The strategies outlined in this book may not be suitable for every individual, and are not meant to provide individualized advice or recommendations.

The advice and strategies found within may not be suitable for every situation. This work is sold with the understanding that neither the author nor the publisher are held responsible for the results accrued from the advice in this book.

All disputes are subject to Delhi jurisdiction only.

# *Dedication*

*Dedicated to my Gurus,*
*my colleagues and my clients*
*who taught me intricacies of finance.*

# *Acknowledgment*

'*Price to Profit*' is my fourth book. You won't know about the other three, because they are as yet unfinished, and will hopefully see light of the day in near future.

Having mastered the art of beginning to write a book, and leaving it half-finished, I could well have continued with it, but for my friend and coach, Kailash Pinjani, who, in his own way, ensured that I complete this book. Another friend and an ace writer himself, Deepak Parbat, guided me in the process.

Developing expertise in pricing needs a solid understanding of accounting, finance and marketing and how these integrate with each other. Three of my professors at IIM Bangalore left deep impression on me during my post-graduation program; Professor S. Sundararajan (accounting), Professor G Sabarinathan (finance) and Professor D V R Seshadri (marketing). I stay indebted to them for their passion and knowledge.

There are a number of fellow professionals who I interacted with, on the topic of pricing. It is difficult to list each of them, but I must mention my friend and IIM Bangalore alumnus, Abhinav Khare, with whom I have had long discussions on pricing strategies.

As a practitioner, I must acknowledge the clients, whose real-life challenges presented me with an opportunity to gain insights that work in practice.

No endeavour can be a success without one's family's complete support. My wife Priya and sons, Pradyumna and Vikrant, encouraged me in this journey, each in their special ways.

Lastly, I received an enthusiastic response to the pre-launch of this book. Besides my friends and associates, a good number of people who I never met, bought this book in the pre-launch offer. They made sure I put in required efforts to make this book as valuable as is possible for me.

Thank you all! Hope you enjoy reading this book, and it benefits you in your business.

# Preface

Over last few years, my interactions with academicians, professionals and entrepreneurs, made me aware that, while businesses are focused on growth, profitability, costs and efficiencies, they are not generally aware of the impact that pricing could have on these goals.

Most entrepreneurs are 'price takers' who accept the price set by the market and generate profits by driving efficiencies and reducing costs. They do not realise the power of pricing, and in case they are aware, do not know which existing strategies they can leverage in their business. Implementing a pricing strategy for a business that is already in existence has its own challenges and complexities.

The goal of writing this book is to create awareness of why pricing is important, how it impacts business growth and profitability, which pricing strategies are being used by businesses, which challenges are faced in implementing pricing strategies, and recommend an approach to execute a pricing strategy in your business.

A single book cannot do justice to a topic as critical and vast as pricing. Each industry has its own structure and intricacies, which call for more detailed discussion on the topic of pricing in that industry. Hopefully this book will set you on a path to discover what works best for your business.

# Foreword

Back in 1980s, while enjoying our college life watching the cricket matches played on the Matunga Gymkhana ground in front of the College, we managed to pass CA examinations and later successfully pursue our respective careers in related fields.

Shailendra was one of the more studious ones of the lot and being consistent with it, he chose to pursue a career in finance, strategy and consulting. So, when I heard about this book-writing endeavour, I was not surprised. As I read through the draft, I found that his studious nature and deep experience in finance was clearly evident in the book.

Pricing is always a complex decision in any organization. All other things being constant, pricing can be the crucial differentiator between a highly profitable business and others. With my 30 years in business management in India and abroad mostly in projects business, I can best vouch for the importance of right pricing for a profitable business. Project pricing is a crucial factor in increasing the chances of a win in a competitive bidding situation.

One may lose the business opportunity by pricing slightly higher or may lose the profit opportunity by pricing very aggressively. Therefore, deciding the right price is always tricky, and the best that one could do is to cover all aspects around pricing.

I find this book especially useful for the ever- growing number of start-ups in Indian landscape. The founders may have an excellent product, but they may not be expert in the market dynamics. A wrong pricing decision may very well render a good product non-sellable or non-profitable, and thus make the business unviable. This book covers all aspects of right pricing and could immensely help them hitting the bullseye of the right pricing for their products. Thus, they can eliminate the blind-spots and increase the chances of building a viable business.

***CA Subodh B Kunte***
*Member of the Board,*
*Executive Director & Chief Financial Officer*
*Primetals Technologies, an MHI group Company*

# Contents

# CHAPTER *One*

## *What is a 'Price'*

*"Price is what you pay. Value is what you get."*

***—Warren Buffett***

Before we get into a deeper discussion on the 'Price', it is imperative that we ask ourselves – what is 'Price'?

## The general conception about a price

Most people, when asked this question, tend to answer that the price is an amount that we receive or pay for a product or service. When we go to a restaurant, the menu lists the price for each item. A tag attached to a shirt or a sweater in a shop mentions an amount, which is a 'Price' of that item. A book has a price mentioned somewhere on the inside cover, or at times on the back cover. This amount is the 'Price' of the item that gets engraved in our mind.

However, in many cases, the tag mentions a "usual price" and "sale price"; which price are we referring to, in that case? We notice this more frequently nowadays when we shop online? There is a price which is displayed as M.R.P. but ~~struck off~~. Then there is a "Price" mentioned which is lower than the M.R.P. To make it even simpler for us, mostly there is a "You Save" amount as well as the percentage specified. Check this price display from one of the famous shopping portals as an example.

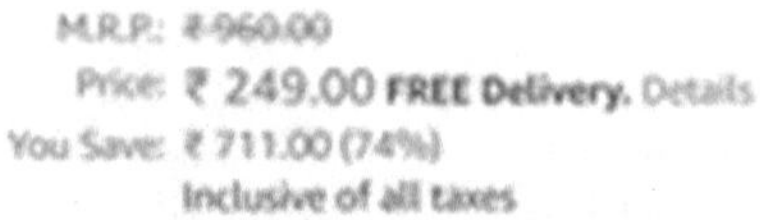

M.R.P.: ~~₹ 960.00~~
Price: ₹ 249.00 FREE Delivery. Details
You Save: ₹ 711.00 (74%)
Inclusive of all taxes

Why is the M.R.P. being displayed along with the current sale price? Why calculate the savings and display the amount of saving, as well as the percentage, if "Price" is simply the amount that we pay?

The above image also shows "free delivery" along with the price. In some cases, the same item is available from multiple sellers. A few sellers include delivery charges in the price, and some a few others quote delivery charges in addition to the 'Price'. Should we not cover the cost of shipment when we calculate the price?

Thus, our understanding of what is a 'Price' gets confusing when we start looking deeper.

## 'Price' in business conversations

In business conversations, the price quoted by the seller is almost always a starting point in the negotiation. However, depending on the complexity of the product, many product features get embedded in the conversation.

The quoted price may be free- on- board (FOB) or for doorstep delivery. There could be optional features for the product, that are quoted separately. There are terms regarding the guarantee and warranty.

The product may come in multiple options, e.g., in terms of the size or capacity. The accuracy levels guaranteed in the output may differ. The buyer, therefore, has a complex task on hand. He has to standardise quotes from multiple vendors and compare them using a standard baseline. While doing so, he has to make certain assumptions and seek clarifications from the vendors to make a comparison across quotes.

## Implications of the general understanding of 'price'

In general, since the customer perceives the monetary amount displayed as "Price" as the price he pays, this acts as a benchmark for comparison between different competing products. The other attributes such as features, shipping costs, packaging, delivery time and warranties do impact the decision-making process. Still, as we can see, these are difficult to benchmark.

How do you, for example, value add additional one-year warranty on a product? Or, for that matter, the features that you may or may not use? Should you put a value on high-resolution camera in a smart-phone when you already have a high-range DSLR? Does it make a difference on your decision if you have purchased that DSLR recently and thus are optimistic that you will use it frequently, against the experience of the majority of the buyers, who continue to use the camera of the smart-phone because of the ease and inevitability of having it in your pocket every time you step out?

Select Your Car

Purchase Price Include potential savings*

All cars have Dual Motor All-Wheel Drive, adaptive air suspension, premium interior and sound

Long Range $77,815*

Performance $97,815*

* Costs above include potential incentives and gas savings of $7,175. Learn More

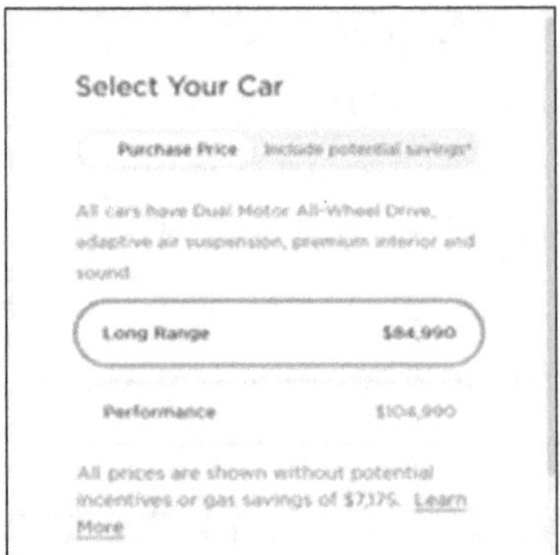


See the above screenshots of the display of the price of a car from one of the automakers, which is considered the most innovative company in various segments. As a default setting, when you review the car, you first see the lower price ($77,815 in this case), which includes potential savings on account of incentives and gas savings. You have to toggle across to see the actual price that you must pay to acquire this car ($84,990 in this case). The company could have chosen to show you the higher price without potential savings first. Still, probably they believe that showing lower price helps them sell more cars. Be assured they must have performed a lot of research using web analytics tools to see which one yields higher sales.

Thus, the general understanding of "Price" being an amount which actually goes out of your pocket (or bank account) when you buy a product is very critical when a customer takes a decision to buy or not buy your product. While trying to differentiate the product on other parameters is also equally important, one should not lose sight of this fact.

## How do we define "Price"?

Taking monetary amount exchanged for acquiring a product alone as a "Price" therefore would amount to taking a narrow view of how the "Price" should be perceived.

*In general terms, Price is the amount that one gives in exchange for something.*

When a customer buys a product, apart from the money paid, there's an expected benefit from the item which implies emotional commitment. A customer won't buy if he is not sure he is making a right choice. More than fear of possible loss of money, the possibility of emotional suffering caused because of a wrong decision, hold people back from buying a product.

If the item is being bought for gifting to someone, there's always an apprehension that if the quality is not right, what would the person receiving the gift think of the person gifting? Thus, while buying something for gifting, the customer would tend to be more cautious. Parents take utmost care while choosing a product for their kids. The younger the children, the more the caution and worry. Thus, the customer tends to buy, depending on the level of trust he has on the seller. More 'established' the brand, higher the level of trust, and hence higher the probability of buying a new product from the same seller.

In a business-to-business transaction, if the item being acquired forms a critical component of the product that the customer sells, the buyer is risking his customer's satisfaction and repeat business while acquiring the component.

One more significant cost that the customer considers while buying is 'time'. When you buy a product, you spend some time using it before you know whether it works for you and gives you the desired benefits. If the product doesn't fit, you have lost valuable time. You may be able to return the product or get compensation or buy another product that works for you. The financial loss may not be significant, but time lost could cost you your reputation.

The relationship between the time commitment the customer has to make (i.e., the time he is likely to commit to losing by buying the product), the trust that puts in you, and the money he would be willing to spend, can be depicted as follows.

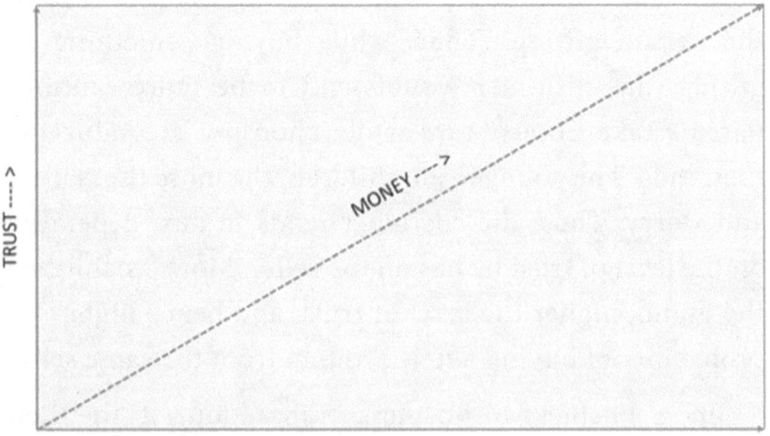

At the beginning of the relationship, the customer would be willing to make less investment of time with you. If he is required to spend a lot of time to confirm correctness of his decision, after buying your product or service, he is less likely to buy the product, unless the trust level is high. You must slowly acquire the trust as well as the confidence of the customer if you want him to spend more money or pay a higher price.

## Why it is critical that we look at the broader aspects beyond the mere quoted price

We must, therefore, consider a more comprehensive view of "Price" beyond the amount mentioned on the tag, for several reasons.

1. **Understand customer buying behaviour and decision making:** While designing a product, the seller looks at the Unique Value proposition (USP), which is about how the product offers benefits that are unique or better than the other competing products. Likewise, while designing the marketing and sales strategy, the seller must understand Unique Buying Points (UBPs). Unique Buying Points should not merely be the USPs turned around and looked at from the customer's point of view. The USPs looked at from the customer's point of view are better called a Customer Value Proposition (CVP). The UBPs are the issues,

obstacles or concerns that the customer must resolve before he or she decides to buy. Do I really need this product? What benefits will it actually deliver? What if I make a wrong decision? Am I wasting my time and money? While resolving UBPs, right price should add weight to the seller's proposition.

2. **Sell more to more customers:** The Second Law: The Law of Compensation from the book "Go-Giver" reads "Your income is determined by how many people you serve and how well you serve them". The more you sell, i.e., the more people you sell to, the more is the opportunity to profit from the sale. Growth attracts capital, motivated employees, innovative and resourceful vendors and so on. The price should enable reaching more extensive number of customers within the target segment.
3. **Get best possible price while delivering highest possible value:** The First Law: The Law of Value from the book "Go-Giver" reads "Your true worth is determined by how much more you give in value than you take in payment". The business that runs profitably over the long run and grows is one which gives more value to the customer than the price it charges. If you provide just adequate value in return for the price, the customer will buy. Still, in the absence of the 'wow' factor, he will quickly switch to another competing product, when the

option is available. This doesn't, however, mean that you charge too less in comparison to the value delivered. The trick is to get the best possible price while providing the best possible value. This is possible only by ensuring that the factors that weigh on the mind of the customer other than price are well understood.

4. **Get repeat business from the same customer:** Number of studies establish that it costs much higher to acquire a new customer than retain and grow an existing customer. It can cost five times more to attract a new customer than it does to retain an existing one. According to Forbes, "increasing customer retention rates by 5% increases profits by 25% to 95%, according to research done by Frederick Reichheld of Bain & Company", and "it can cost five times more to attract a new customer than it does to retain an existing one". <Reference> Understanding the factors that influence customer's decision beyond the price is important for retaining the customer and selling him more of the same product, or cross-selling other products to him.

*"Pricing is the exchange rate you put on all the tangible and intangible aspects of your business. Value for cash."*

***—Patrick Campbell***

## Reference

https://www.forbes.com/sites/jiawertz/2018/09/12/dont-spend-5-times-more-attracting-new-customers-nurture-the-existing-ones/#13e7b4695a8e

# CHAPTER *Two*

## *Price = Growth + Profitability*

*"The moment you make a mistake in pricing, you're eating into your reputation or your profits."*

***—Katharine Paine***

In the previous chapter, we looked at why we must look at the 'price' holistically. Unfortunately, if you observe entrepreneurs in action, you will, for sure, find that most of the business conversations and efforts are focused on cutting costs, and not improving pricing power. Let's now look at why pricing a product or service appropriately is key to business growth and profitability.

## Why focus on pricing

Fundamentally, every business makes profit by producing goods or services at a particular cost and selling those to the customers at a price which is higher than the cost. In the example that follows, the costs are classified under direct costs and indirect costs. The direct costs are incurred to produce the goods and services, while indirect costs are incurred towards selling, general and administration. Most of the direct costs change with the level of change in production, whereas indirect costs remain stable. In practice, direct costs may not change directly in proportion to the level of production for various reasons. In specific cases, such as an information technology product, the same product code is reused for a new customer while incurring negligible costs. Likewise, in practice, the indirect costs also change, such as higher investment in sales and marketing teams for expansion in new markets. However, for the simplicity of driving home the point, it is assumed that the direct costs change with the level of production, whereas indirect costs remain the same.

## Pricing has a direct impact on profitability

| | *Base case* | *Cost Reduction* | *Price Increase* | *Price Increase + Cost Reduction* |
|---|---|---|---|---|
| Price | 100 | 100 | 110 | 110 |
| Direct costs | 40 | 36 | 40 | 36 |
| Indirect costs | 50 | 50 | 50 | 50 |
| Profit | 10 | 14 | 20 | 24 |
| Profit Margin | 10% | 14% | 18% | 22% |

In the base case, the profit margin is 10% on the price of Rs 100.

If the entrepreneur focuses on the cost reduction (as is seen to be the general tendency), he may be able to bring a specific saving by measures such as:

1. Improving employee productivity through training and incentives- in which case the part of gains

from increased productivity will be lost in training costs and incentives

2. Procuring raw material and other supplies from the vendors at reduced rates. This can be achieved by ordering materials in large quantity for trade or volume discounts; in which case the costs of carrying inventory will absorb some of the costs saved. Alternative vendors can be explored and tapped, which may lead to quality issues, till the vendors prove their reliability. If the vendors are forced to negotiate and supply at a low rate, they may agree, but give preference to other customers, or may compromise on quality or supply schedule. The credit period extended by the vendors may have to be reduced to compensate for lower rates.

Thus, cost reduction comes at the cost of potentially unhappy employees or vendors, unless it is made through genuine and long-lasting productivity increase.

In the above example, by reducing direct costs by 10% (from Rs. 40 to Rs. 36), the profit is increased to Rs. 14 or 14% on the sale price of Rs. 100.

Instead of focusing on cost reduction, if the entrepreneur manages to increase the price by 10%, from Rs. 100 to Rs. 110, the entire increase of Rs. 10 flows to the bottom line. This has the potential to double the profit from Rs. 10 to Rs. 20 and improve the profit margin from 10% to 18%.

In the best possible scenario, if the entrepreneur manages to do both, i.e., reduce the cost by 10%, as well as increase the price by 10%, the profit can be considerably improved from Rs. 10 to Rs. 24, and the margin from 10% to 22%.

While these scenarios may look simplistic, the fundamental point I would like to drive is that pricing decision is as essential, or at times, more important than the costs, and hence must receive lot of attention from the entrepreneur.

*Change in prices have a considerable impact on growth and profitability.*

*"The impact of the price is always greater than that of the other three profit drivers, i.e., sales volume, fixed costs, and variable costs."*

***—E J Bouter***

## Pricing has a direct impact on growth

One of the mistakes many entrepreneurs make is that they have a single price for their product. While this may perfectly fit the customers' needs and thus make sense, this also means he is leaving out those customers who want the similar product and have different spending power. The product price may not appeal to a wealthy customer and may be unaffordable for someone who has relatively less spending power.

Let's look at a hypothetical example of an entrepreneur having a single product priced at Rs. 10,000 per unit. The entrepreneur has forecasted the sales and revenue as follows.

| ***Base case*** | | | | | | | |
|---|---|---|---|---|---|---|---|
| ***Product*** | ***Price*** | | ***Year 1*** | ***Year 2*** | ***Year 3*** | ***Year 4*** | ***Year 5*** |
| Standard | 10000 | Qty sold | 5000 | 6000 | 7200 | 8650 | 10400 |
| Revenue | | Rs lakhs | 500 | 600 | 720 | 865 | 1040 |

In this case, the projected growth in unit sales and revenue is 20% year on year.

For Rs. 10,000 customers who have higher spending power may be left out, because the product design and packaging may not attract them, or they may want an additional feature which is "exclusive". Likewise, some of the potential buyers may like the product, but can't afford to pay Rs. 10,000. They may be willing to buy the product at a lower price, and in return, settle for a relatively simpler design, simple packaging and non-availability of feature/s that they can manage without.

To tap those potential buyers, if say, three versions of the same product are introduced, with distinctive features and different prices, it may be possible to generate higher revenues.

| ***Choice - scenario 1 - same qty sold*** | | | | | | | |
|---|---|---|---|---|---|---|---|
| ***Product*** | ***Price*** | | ***Year 1*** | ***Year 2*** | ***Year 3*** | ***Year 4*** | ***Year 5*** |
| Silver | 7500 | Qty sold | 1000 | 1200 | 1440 | 1730 | 2080 |
| Gold | 12500 | Qty sold | 3500 | 4200 | 5040 | 6055 | 7280 |
| Platinum | 15000 | Qty sold | 500 | 600 | 720 | 865 | 1040 |
| All versions | | | 5000 | 6000 | 7200 | 8650 | 10400 |
| Revenue | | Rs. lakhs | 588 | 705 | 846 | 1016 | 1222 |

The example above assumes the projected growth in unit sales of 20% year on year, which is similar to the base case.

However, since the product is now priced differently for the three customer segments, there is higher revenue as compared to the base case. The 'platinum' version of the product may have exactly the same specifications that the standard product earlier had, however, the premium customers will now find the product more attractive in *comparison* to the other two versions. The increase in price from Rs. 10,000 to Rs. 15,000 will also make it possible to add distinctive feature/s that otherwise could not be added to the standard product due to cost considerations, thus increasing the appeal further. Likewise, the potential buyers who liked the product but could not afford it for Rs. 10,000, can now buy the "silver" version of the product at Rs. 7,500. The "silver" version may have a few features less, and relatively inexpensive packaging etc.

Now, let's look at what more this strategy may yield. By pricing the product versions at different points, it is likely that a potential competitor who wants to bring in a competing low-priced product, will not be able to design, build or market the same actively and take away market share.

| ***Choice - scenario 2 - more qty sold*** | | | | | | | |
|---|---|---|---|---|---|---|---|
| Silver | 7500 | Qty sold | 1200 | 1500 | 1880 | 2350 | 2940 |
| Gold | 12500 | Qty sold | 4200 | 5250 | 6580 | 8225 | 10290 |
| Platinum | 15000 | Qty sold | 600 | 750 | 940 | 1175 | 1470 |
| All versions | | | 6000 | 7500 | 9400 | 11750 | 14700 |
| Revenue | | Rs lakhs | 705 | 881 | 1105 | 1381 | 1727 |

The example above assumes the projected growth in unit sales of 25% year on year, which is higher than the previous two cases. The three segments are likely to potentially offer more conversions from prospects to customers because of the broader target market.

This higher growth in unit sales translated into higher revenue. Over five years, compared to the base case, the income is

- 18% higher in the second case ("Choice - scenario 1 - same qty sold"), and
- 56% higher in the latter case ("Choice - scenario 2 - more qty sold").

While these scenarios are hypothetical, this demonstrates the possibilities that creative pricing can open up. Look around, and you will find mobile phones, cars, theatre seats, printers, air conditioners, washing machines, and every other product marketer using this strategy. Why shouldn't you?

*"If you've got the power to raise prices without losing business to a competitor, you've got a great business. And if you have to have a prayer session before raising the price by 10 per cent, then you've got a terrible business."*

***—Warren Buffett***

# CHAPTER *Three*

## *Importance of Pricing*

*"Pricing power is the single most important decision in evaluating a business."*

***—Warren Buffett***

In the previous chapter, we looked at how appropriate pricing can help boost revenues as well as profitability. These two twin goals of growing business and running it profitability are top goals for every business entrepreneur, and hence he can't afford to ignore the criticality of pricing.

E J Bouter, in his book, "Pricing: The Third Business Skill- Principles of rice Management", adds "pricing" as the third business skill that an entrepreneur must have, besides the skills of an inventor and the salesman

The strong positive relationship between pricing power, growth and profitability is a result of a number of signals that a product price sends out. The pricing strategy is vital for the following reasons.

1. Pricing is Positioning
2. Price defines competition
3. Pricing is key to target the right customer segment
4. Price helps attract and qualify the right customer
5. The right price is key to extracting right value of the product

6. Price serves as an indicator of quality
7. Right price helps win new business
8. Price must recover rising costs from inflation
9. Price is critical for sustaining the business

Let's look at each of these reasons.

## 1. Pricing is Positioning

In marketing parlance, the business or product 'positioning' is the positioning in the mind of the customer. Primarily, positioning is about "the place a brand occupies in the mind of its target audience". It doesn't matter what the entrepreneur thinks about his business. It doesn't matter what the investors or employees think of the business. What matters is what the customers think of the business or a product.

How you price your product conveys your 'positioning' to the customer. A product that seeks to be perceived as a 'premium' product must always be priced higher. There's no exception to this rule.

A Jaguar or a Maybach can't be priced the same as most of the Toyota models. A potential buyer, in most cases, can't technically evaluate the product. At the same time, he or she may boast so, using the jargon used by the "industry experts" while assessing the products.

*"Pricing is branding."*

***—Richie Norton***

This rule is universally applicable. Be it watches (number of Swiss brands), laptops, mobile phones and tablets (Apple), or a Whiskey (Scotch). Most of these products cost the same to produce and distribute, as compared to the other "non-premium" brands. The additional benefits that they offer are, at times, pure illusion or have a real minor use. How many of us have dropped a phone for a long time in water and tested waterproof characteristics? How many of us can drink a Whiskey from a crystal Whiskey decanter and identify a brand? Nevertheless, when packaged and branded, we end up paying 2x or 10x price and boast it in from of friends (and enemies).

This is not so to say that a Jaguar car or an Omega watch doesn't deliver any superior benefits over the lower-priced competing products. They do. However, these benefits are not easily identifiable or are not material enough to matter to most of us. Possessing these brands, however, sends a "signal" to others, about your wealth and "status".

If a premium product is priced lower, it may lose most of its attraction for the buyers. Simply stated, it will lose its premium "positioning" in the mind of the buyers. This position is not acquired easily; it takes a lot of efforts and creative marketing to achieve that status. Even an industrial group as old, large, well established and prestigious as Tatas find it challenging to position their watches on par with some of the iconic Swiss brands, after spending top budgets.

Thus, while setting the price, entrepreneur must carefully consider where he wants to position his business and the product.

## 2. Price defines competition

'Positioning' also refers to the place that a brand occupies in the minds of the customers and how it is distinguished from the products of the competitors. Besides occupying a distinct place in the minds of the customers, by positioning a product, the entrepreneur also defines who his competitors are.

A restaurant is a place that serves food and charges money for it. Regardless of which restaurant you go to and which type of food it serves, once you have consumed it, the effect is the same as having had food in another restaurant. Thus, every restaurant is, by definition, open to competition from all the restaurants in the nearby vicinity. The cuisine served is, of course, one of the differentiators. However, will the restaurant consider every other restaurant as its competitor?

The other factors that differentiate the restaurant come into play. Besides location and cuisine, the ambience, the hygiene and the service are usual differentiators. The restaurant-aggregator and food delivery websites and apps specifically highlight how much a "meal for two" costs. This indication segregates the restaurants for the customer, who is ordering food from the comfort of his home. He is not going to experience the service and ambience of the restaurant; hence the price becomes a distinctive criterion to arrive at a decision.

## 3. Pricing is key to target the right customer segment

Peter Drucker, one of the most widely known and influential thinkers on management, mentioned "seeking high-profit margins and premium pricing" as one of the 5 marketing sins. The other sins include "charging what the market will bear" and "using cost-driven pricing".

Drucker's problem with premium pricing was on two accounts:

1. Premium pricing leaves out a large segment of the market, and therefore may go against the goal of profit maximization and
2. Premium pricing leaves the door open for competition for lower-end competitors

The entrepreneur is, accordingly, essentially segmenting the market when he takes a pricing decision. The lower-end competitors leave out the high-end affluent buyers, whereas premium positioning leaves out the mass-market at the lower end. If the messaging through price is not clear, you may attract a lot of prospects; however, the conversions will be lower.

A Harley Davidson or a BMW bike is not priced for the customer who looks at a bike as a means of moving from one place to another. The Bajaj bike of 100 cc is targeted at a cost-conscious customer who uses the bike as a means of daily commute. Whereas, a Bajaj Pulsar 150 cc targets an aspirational youth (mostly male), who wants a feel of a powerful bike at a price he can afford. Pulsar, therefore, comes in a price range where the higher end is 2x the lower end, thus casting the net as wide as practical.

While the customer doesn't buy solely based on price, the price makes him quickly narrow down the competing alternatives and thus makes his decision making easy. Someone looking for a cost-effective means of transport won't waste his time on Harley Davidson or a BMW, or even on a Bajaj Pulsar. Looking at it from the seller's point of view, they get the right customer in the showroom, and the salesperson's time is spent productively, increasing the conversions.

## 4. Price helps attract and qualify the right customer

By segmenting the customer and positioning the product through pricing, a seller narrows down the competition and crafts his marketing message accordingly to stand out from the narrowly defined competition. However, not every business wants to exclude specific segments of the customer.

Let's take an example of a mall or a departmental store (multi-brand, multi-product retailer). They would like to get as many potential buyers in the outlet or on the eCommerce portal and offer them an as wide a choice as possible. This, however, means it is difficult to identify the buyer's decision as well as the paying capacity.

Having got the footfalls into the mall or eyeballs to the portal, the next step would be to ensure that the buyer is easily able to identify what suits his needs and choose accordingly. The customer should, therefore, be easily able to narrow done the range of products that suit his requirement and budget. This is done by segregating products by category or display sections, and putting additional attractions like 'introductory discount', 'one-for-one free', or clearance sale' or its equivalent, to suit the specific customer within the target segment.

## 5. The right price is key to extracting right value of the product

While one must make every attempt to provide maximum value to the customer at the best possible price, one should also check whether the price is proportionate to the value delivered. If you charge too low, or too high, compared to the value delivered, the customer may either perceive that the product is of low quality, or that you are trying to extract too much. In both cases, the customer will look for an appropriately priced product that deliver the right value.

The Chinese cars started selling in Australia around 2009, but after almost 10 years, as of 2018, they have been able to capture only less than 1% of the market share. Most analysts had predicted that the Chinese carmakers would catch up with the Korean counterparts in 5 to 10 years; however, they have been wrong. The new brands on Chinese cars were priced way below the other brands, but that created doubts in the minds of the car buyers regarding quality and safety. Over the period, these are being resolved through higher ratings in car crash tests, but the market share is expanding slowly. Probably Chinese carmakers should have invested more in safety and in providing quality assurance, at a price was not too low, to capture market share early on.

*"Find the right price for an irresistible offer, which, by the way, isn't necessarily the lower price."*

***—W. Chan Kim***

If you don't extract the right value for the product, you will not get enough surplus to invest in innovation to keep making the product better.

## 6. Price serves as an indicator of quality

A product priced very low usually calls into question the quality of the product. This is for a reason. Ensuring quality requires procuring best quality of input materials, adherence to process, use of right tools and techniques, appointing inspectors or their machine counterparts who perform quality checks, and investing in marketing to convey the customers the story behind the product.

If you buy a product because it is priced low and then later discover that the quality is terrible, this gets imprinted on the memory. Any possible savings made from buying low are soon forgotten.

*"The bitterness of poor quality remains long after low pricing is forgotten!"*

***—Leon M. Cautillo***

*"Quality is remembered long after the price is forgotten"*

***—Gucci Family Slogan***

Toyota, for example, is perceived by car owners as a car that has high quality. This reflects the overall low cost of ownership over the lifetime of the car. Toyota car models like Qualis, Etios and Innova had a significant market share of private taxi segment in India for years, because the taxi- owners swear by the Toyota's engine quality and that it sold for a reasonable price even after running 3 lakh kilometres. Likewise, Toyota Corolla and Camry dominated taxi segment in Singapore for long. This was achieved, besides quality, through appropriately pricing these cars in the mid-range as compared to the competition.

## 7. Right price helps win new business

The end goal of pricing exercising is to ensure that the sale is made. The pricing strategy cannot exist in isolation and work unless customers buy the product. Hence the price must be a "winning" price.

The "winnable" price assumes significance in business – to -business deals when the customer is convinced that the product or service meets his needs, and wants to buy, subject to meeting his expectations on the price. In many cases, the buyer on the customer side indicates the budget that is available for purchase. This sets the upper limit on the deal value. Any amount over the budget will meet stiff resistance from the customer's decision-makers. Hence it comes to a deal or no-deal situation.

In this situation, a clever salesperson has to balance the expectations of his organization and the expectations of the customer. Can he negotiate a bigger deal with a partial commitment right now for the current budgetary period? Can he unbundle the offer and see what best he can offer to the customer given the budgetary constraint? Is there a competitor who the customer is negotiating with? What deal is the competitor likely to offer? How much scope for negotiation was there when the first quote was given? What is the opportunity for cross-sell and up-sell with the customer?

Pricing the offering or a product to close the deal is most critical in such scenarios. And the price quoted should leave scope for the salesperson to try best to offer a winnable price.

## 8. Price must recover rising costs from inflation

Inflation is a given in most economies that grow. During the last few decades, some of the developed economies have had deficient levels of inflation. A few like Japan have near-zero to zero inflation. However, this is still not a norm.

Year on year inflation is bound to add to the cost of producing and delivering products and services in the future. Hence price must be flexible enough to accommodate future increased costs. This is especially relevant for long-term contracts for executing projects, or for the supply of products, or rendering services.

Some of the product vendors provide long-term license renewals, annual maintenance contracts (AMCs), warranties and support. At times, these are priced as a percentage of the upfront amount charged to the customer. A classic example of this would be license renewals, AMCs and support contracts provided by the IT application providers, such as ERP companies. Another example is the pricing committed by the providers of Software as a Service (SaaS) or Platform as a Service (PaaS) providers.

The costs of providing product enhancements, bug fixes, technology upgrade, and support and maintenance are bound to rise over the years, unless the product is of nature which won't need such costs to be incurred at all. The price linked to the original cost of acquisition by the customer (e.g., connected to one-time upfront licensing cost) through a percentage, will not be able to accommodate the increased costs of providing these services oner the years.

Thus, having reset clauses that revise upwards the costs of providing such services in future must be incorporated in the contract. In their absence, subsequent negotiations with the customers will receive a pushback and damage goodwill.

## 9. Price is critical for sustaining the business

Businesses that support and grow over long-term tend to have a healthy profitability and cash flows. With fast changes in lifestyle and technology, most products undergo massive changes over a decade. Making those changes to the product needs investment of time and money. Unless the company has a pricing strategy that keeps generating the profits and cash flows over the years, product innovation is not possible.

The product that goes through classic phases of a product lifecycle, viz., research and development, growth, maturity and decline, will tend to put the organization also on the path to decline, unless the 'decline' phase is arrested through continuous innovation.

*"This thing called 'price' is really, really important. I still think that a lot of people under-think it through. You have a lot of companies that start, and the only difference between the ones that succeed and fail is that one figured out how to make money because they were deep-in thinking through the revenue, price, and business model. I think that's under-attended to generally."*

***—Steve Ballmer***

# CHAPTER *Four*

## *Assess Your Current Pricing Strategy*

*"The market is like Goldilocks. It decides if your price is too hot, too cold, or just right."*

***—Peter F Porcelli Jr***

If you are currently running a business, it is imperative that you evaluate your current pricing strategy. This would help identify areas where there is a scope for improvement.

A few areas which should be evaluated include

1. Identification of customer segments
2. Choice of marketing and sales channels
3. Cost of customer acquisition
4. Quantifying customer value delivered
5. Forecasted Cash flows and budgets
6. Offering risk- reward-based solution
7. Deep understanding of product benefits
8. Product and solution variants
9. Resolving customer buying objections
10. Demonstrating confidence in the product

## Pricing Strategy Analysis Questionnaire

Let's look at a questionnaire design to assess the current pricing strategy. If you are currently running a business, award yourself a score between 0 to 10 for each of the questions below, where '0' indicates a clear "No", and '10' a clear "Yes". Use your judgment to award a '0'0, '10', or any score in-between on that scale.

| *Sr No* | *Parameter* | *Score* |
|---|---|---|
| | Do you have distinct criteria for pricing for B2B and B2C segments? | |
| | Do you have distinct criteria for pricing for each channel, e.g., digital/ others | |
| | Do you assess the cost of customer acquisition while setting a price? | |
| | Do you demonstrate ROI for the client? | |
| | Do you calibrate the impact of price changes on profits and cash flows? | |
| | Do you link your prices to customer business goals and growth? | |
| | Do you use key product features to distinguish product versions? | |
| | Do you provide multiple product variants as a part of your offering? | |
| | Do you guarantee product returns based on measurable performance criteria? | |
| | Do you offer a free trial to the customers to demonstrate product utility? | |
| | Total score out of 100 | |

## 1. Identification of customer segments

*Do you have distinct criteria for pricing for B2B and B2C segments?*

In marketing jargon, the customer segments are broadly classified into Business to Business (B2B) and Business to Consumer (B2C). B2B transaction involves the product being consumed by an organisation which sells its products to another business (B2B0 or eventually to the consumers (B2C). Whereas, the products sold via B2C channel are directly consumed, thus ending the value-chain.

Over a while, businesses have evolved into more matured and meaningful identification of channels into those that make sense to them from their point of view. A branded quick-service restaurant can now serve food at own outlet (B2C), through a franchise (B2F2C), through a food aggregator like Swiggy or Uber Eats (B2A2C), to a Corporate for their event (B2B), or to a Corporate event through an Event Partner (B2E2B), and so on. A manufacturer of Indian masalas may sell directly to consumers at the factory store or own retail outlet (B2C), through an Institution like Canteen Stores Department (CSD) of Indian armed forces (B2I2C), or through an eCommerce player like Amazon (B2e2C) and so on.

It is imperative that the entrepreneur understand the buyer motivation and behaviour while choosing a channel of purchase, in addition to the channel reach, appeal, customer segmentation, cross-selling opportunities, channel commissions and other charges like logistics costs, tax implications, offers and discounts strategy, and typical purchase quantity etc. The gross prices (or MRP –

maximum retail price), taxes, channel-specific prices and delivery options are designed accordingly.

The products that are delivered over the internet (e.g., e-books, online courses, webinars, Software as a Service (SaaS) applications involve no additional cost of delivering to a new customer. The product is built and ready to consume. Their pricing is therefore, distinct from the physically delivered products.

The critical question that the entrepreneur should answer is whether he is aware of the nuances of each channel and able to price the product accordingly.

## 2. Choice of marketing and sales channels

*Do you have distinct criteria for pricing for each channel, e.g., digital/ others*

Number of channels available for selling products and services have increased over decades. In the last two decades, digital channels increased and added to the complexities involved.

Marketplaces like Amazon, Flipkart and eBay today represent a high share of sales for several products. Some of the businesses rely on these channels almost exclusively. It is at times more comfortable selling through an online B2C marketplace than establish your marketing, sales, and distribution machinery. The products delivered to the consumer via a simple supply chain comprising manufacturer - wholesaler/ distributor - retailer model can now be sold nationwide using an online marketplace.

The channels cater not only to the traditional products but have opened up newer avenues of producing the product itself. Books don't have to be necessarily hardcover or paperback now, but you can download it on Kindle using wireless or phone data.

If you sell across various channels, you must follow pricing that adapts to the complexities of the channel. This is essential so that you can protect your margins while maximising sales. However, there are challenges involved in pricing, some of which are listed below.

1. *Reach:* Each channel's capability to reach the target audience could be different. The reach may differ by demographics (e.g., age or language), literacy levels, interest areas, and income level. Likewise, the deal size may vary based on the target profile reached.
2. *Scalability:* The reach, as well as the ability of each channel to handle volumes, is different. Sale at factory door cuts down on margins of the intermediaries as well as the logistic costs. However, getting the customer to the factory may need a significant spend on the marketing. Also, the scale may not be achieved since the customers expect convenience.

3. *Conversions:* The conversion rate across channels is not the same. A salesman at a store has a much better chance of engaging the customer, resolving the queries and use his sales skills to convert a prospect into a customer. A prospect browsing Facebook is likely to click through to the desired landing page if his interest area matches the target profile; the chances of his conversion into a customer are high if the target profile is mapped well to the product.
4. *Channel commissions:* Each channel has its commission model. The rates as well the modalities of calculation may vary. Amazon, for example, charges their "fees" as a percentage depending on the product category, and a flat- fees (closure charges) for each deal. The wholesalers charge their commissions which may go up to 40% in some cases, where they have a stronghold on the distribution network.
5. *Taxes and other costs:* Other costs involved in reaching the customer include taxes and duties, such as GST on commissions. Additionally, the marketing, advertising, and content development professionals' costs are involved.

In a multi-channel sales model, using the same price across channels is a sure recipe for disaster. It is essential, therefore that a business develops a pricing model that helps achieve business goals across channels. The model should be simple enough for everyone in the organisation to understand and easy to use. The model should be flexible enough to be changed as the market changes. It should be possible to validate results and perform ack-testing. On top of all this, the model should help focus on key business goals of growth in sales, maintaining the desired level of profitability and operating an efficient cash cycle.

## 3. Cost of customer acquisition

*Do you assess the cost of customer acquisition while setting a price?*

The cost of acquiring customer includes various components such as the cost of the branding exercise, advertising, sales, events, channel costs and referral bonuses to the customers. The cost of acquiring a customer through each of these channels could be different. In most businesses, this cost is, indeed, changed.

An example of the cost of customer acquisition is given below.

| *Channel* | *Budget Rs* | *Targets Reached Nos* | *Conversion %* | *Customers Acquired Nos* | *Cost of Acquisition Rs* |
|---|---|---|---|---|---|
| **Digital Marketing** | | | | | |
| Google Campaign Management fees | | | | | |
| YouTube influencers' fees | | | | | |

| Channel | Budget Rs | Targets Reached Nos | Conversion % | Customers Acquired Nos | Cost of Acquisition Rs |
|---|---|---|---|---|---|
| Facebook advertisement fees | | | | | |
| LinkedIn advertisement fees | | | | | |
| | | | | | |
| **Traditional Channels** | | | | | |
| Direct Marketing - Corporate Events | | | | | |
| Direct Marketing - Street Campaigns | | | | | |
| Direct Marketing - Apartment Events | | | | | |
| Advertisements - Newspapers | | | | | |
| Advertisements - TV | | | | | |
| Advertisements - Radio | | | | | |
| | | | | | |
| **Partner Channels** | | | | | |
| Public Relations - Newspaper Partnerships | | | | | |
| Fusion Marketing - Channel Partners | | | | | |
| Outbound Leads Generators | | | | | |
| industry Marketing - Events & Exhibitions | | | | | |

| *Channel* | *Budget Rs* | *Targets Reached Nos* | *Conversion %* | *Customers Acquired Nos* | *Cost of Acquisition Rs* |
|---|---|---|---|---|---|
| Distributors & Wholesalers | | | | | |
| Customer- Friends & Family Referrals | | | | | |
| | | | | | |
| **Onboarding costs** | | | | | |
| Payment gateway costs | | | | | |
| Customer Onboarding support | | | | | |
| | | | | | |
| **Outbound Sales** | | | | | |
| Executives | | | | | |
| Team Leads | | | | | |
| | | | | | |
| **Total Customer Acquisition Costs** | | | | | |

The cost of customer acquisition should be compared with potential revenue through various channels, customer retention rates and the potential profitability and accordingly allocate the budget to a channel.

## 4. Quantifying customer value delivered

*Do you demonstrate ROI for the client?*

In the business- to- business segment, the products sold to the customers form a part of the product or service that the customers sell to their customers, either directly or indirectly. Thus, the customer would like to buy a product that helps get as high a return on the investment made in purchasing the product, as possible.

If the product is priced higher than the competitor's product, one of the best ways to still ensure that the customer reviews you offer to demonstrate how overall cost of your product (total cost of ownership and usage) is lower than the competitor's, this could be on account of a lower cost of training in usage, lower repairs and maintenance cost, lower downtime, and so on. On the other hand, the return that the customer gets in terms of benefits delivered, higher productivity, increase in the perceived value of the end product, the higher price of the end product, lower cost of servicing the end product, and so on, could be higher.

*"Price is very rarely the reason why our customers don't buy. We have to be honest with ourselves and realise that we failed to show them the value that our product has. Increase value and price becomes secondary."*

***—Nick Stringari***

Most laptops and PCs come with a prominent label "intel inside' displayed on the packaging as well the laptop or PC itself. This is because, Intel has over the years built an image in the mind of the users, that a computer with Intel processor gives better performance compared to other processors. This, in turn, helps sell the laptop or PC at a higher price.

To demonstrate the ROI from your product to the customer, you must understand customers' business well, besides recognising what value the customers deliver to their customers. When you work the numbers, and they are credible, the customer understands that you know their business very well, which helps in closing the deal at a better price. Therefore, a company that can confidently demonstrate the ROI for the customer has a better prospect.

## 5. Forecasted Cash flows and budgets

*Do you calibrate the impact of price changes on profits and cash flows?*

As we discussed in chapter 2 "Price = Growth + Profitability", the product price has a direct impact on revenues, profitability and cash flows.

Any change in price must be made after carefully modelling the impact of the switch on the revenue, profitability and cash flows. Based on my experience, most micro, small and medium business do not have an updated financial model that they can use for calibrating the change and its impact. Moreover, the companies do not model the critical decisions they take frequently, e.g., pricing projects they bid for, special offers, festival sales, the impact of foreign exchange rate movement, change in terms of the franchise agreement and so on. These have a considerable impact, some of which is visible only a few quarters after implementing the changes.

See the example below to understand how a 3% reduction in royalty on prices charged by a quick-service restaurant (QSR) franchise' can reduce the profits of the franchise' owner by 37%.

| | *Scenario A* | *Scenario B* | *Scenario C* |
|---|---|---|---|
| Franchise revenues | 100 | 100 | 100 |
| GST at 5% (no input credit) | 5% | 5% | 5% |
| Net franchise revenues for royalty | 95 | 95 | 95 |
| Cost of production and delivery to franchise | 40 | 40 | 40 |
| Gross Margin on items sold to franchise | 33% | 33% | 33% |
| Franchise royalty %age | 10% | 9% | 7% |
| Indirect costs and management overhead | 15 | 15 | 15 |
| Net profit from franchise operations | 7.70 | 6.75 | 4.85 |

## 6. Offering risk- reward-based solution

*Do you link your prices to customer business goals and growth?*

If you understand your customer's business, their challenges and value drivers well, you should be able to understand the risks and rewards in the customer's business, that is likely to be impacted from using your product.

If you are willing to share risk in customer's business (e.g., lower growth in the market), and in return demand a higher price as a reward for the same, you move from being a 'vendor' to be a 'trusted partner'. Most customers are willing to pay higher if they are, in turn, able to make higher sales and profits. Linking your business success to the customer's helps get higher sales and better price.

## 7. Deep understanding of product benefits

*Do you use key product features to distinguish product versions?*

Though this may appear surprising to some, many entrepreneurs fail to conduct a more in-depth analysis of their products and services to understand what features they can separately identify. This is essential for you to compare your product, its benefits, value delivered, and relative price as compared to the competitor's products and services.

If the product is used by an average non-technical user, the features can be categorised into those that are

1. Highly technical features which user may not understand or base his decision upon
2. Technical features that can be explained in natural language to impress users
3. Non-technical features that are of real benefit to the user

4. Non-technical features that are inconsequential from user's point of view

The product features under 2 and 3 above should be listed and used to explain the comparative advantages of the product over the competitor's product. These features can be combined to create different product features to manage costs and charge different prices.

## 8. Product and solution variants

*Do you provide multiple product variants as a part of your offering?*

Every product caters to some of the needs of the customers and solves a problem that the customer faces. However, while the question or need is the same for different customers at a high level, if we carefully analyse, each customer's need may differ to a certain extent.

Take an example of an entrepreneur looking for a tool to create a website on their own. Wix.com, one of the leading website builders, provides plans across two main categories, viz., (i) website plans, and (ii) business and eCommerce plans. Within each of these categories, there are a couple of plans that provide increasing features and functionalities for a progressively higher price. Since the needs of the specific entrepreneur are unique, he will choose the most appropriate option. If these options were not available with Wix.com, he would look for options available from the competitors of Wix.com.

Thus, having multiple variants for the same product provides a broader choice to the customer, and the customer can pay the price equivalent to the value the product delivers. This helps capture a much broader base, thus broadening the target market, comprising of the customers with varying capacity to pay, and diverse needs.

## 9. Resolving customer buying objections

*Do you guarantee product returns based on measurable performance criteria?*

A customer who has no previous business relationship, or an existing customer, who has not bought the product from you, may understandably have genuine concerns about the usefulness of the product, specific to his needs. This leads to indecisiveness and delay in the buying decision. Moreover, the customer may be using alternative vendor, which works for him. Thus, he may find a risk in switching to your product.

One of the ways of getting over this concern of the customer is to assure that you are willing to accept the product back and pay back the money to the customer. Most leading eCommerce portals nowadays today offer no-questions-asked returns. They may restrict the number of items for which this return option is available or may make it possible to select customers. The reason is there are substantial costs involved in processing returns, that include the product being physically accepted back.

The money-back-guarantee can also be offered for services. However, the provider should be careful who this guarantee is being provided to, because unscrupulous customers may avail the service, and ask for the money-back. However, there is a consensus that if you have good enough mechanism in place to attract the right customers, the problem rarely occurs.

In a business-to-business transaction, this may help the decision-maker in the customer's organisation handle the objections of the gatekeepers and distractors. The money-back-guarantee, however, can't take away the time risk of the customer, i.e., the risk that the customer will lose time by later having to go for the competing product.

You should find out the customer's expectations on the product's performance which may weight in his mind while making the decision. The money-back-guarantee may be given based on some measurable performance criteria that is of importance to the customer, e.g., 99.9% uptime of infrastructure.

## 10. Demonstrating confidence in the product

*Do you offer a free trial to the customers to demonstrate product utility?*

Offering free trial to the customer is almost the same as giving a no-questions-asked money-back guarantee. The customers would prefer a free trial over the money-back guarantee because no money is at risk.

Trial period is very popular in products such as the off-the-shelf software solutions since the delivery and deployment of such products doesn't involve complexities and requires minimum costs. E.g., the anti-virus solution providers typically provide one-month free usage. After the trial period, the customer has to either pay for the license to use or discontinue. Several products offer a free trial of a basic version of the product and charge for the 'premium' version, which has additional features that a professional` user needs.

Even a sweets seller offers the test of the product (a trial) to the customer by allowing them to test small portions. On Whiskey trail in the Scottish Highlands, you get to taste many whiskies before deciding to buy (or not buy). Wherever, experiencing the product is critical before making the decision to buy, offering a free trial is a good strategy if the seller has confidence in the utility of the product.

*"Cost is of no importance in setting the price.*
*It only helps you to know whether you should be*
*making the product."*

***—Philip Kotler***

# CHAPTER *Five*

## *Impact of Pricing on Strategic Decisions*

*"You don't sell through price. You sell the price."*

***—Philip Kotler***

Pricing strategy is an intrinsic part of the business strategy, since it has a direct bearing on crucial business areas. These business areas include:

1. Product design: customer-centric design, versioning
2. Marketing: Segmenting customers, choosing channels and assessing demand
3. Customer acquisition: Channel optimisation, cost of customer acquisition
4. Selling: Designing sales commissions, offers and discounts and sales pitch
5. Funding: Business plan and forecasting for raising funds, business valuation
6. Investing: Investing in assets, undertaking new projects or acquiring a business
7. Revenues: Revenue earning products, marketing funnel, conversions
8. Profitability: Managing gross margins and net margins
9. Managing costs: Managing fixed, variable and semi-variable costs, the break-even point

10. Planning taxes: GST and other taxes
11. Cash flows: Cash flows and cash budgeting
12. Return on Investment (ROI): Business model, build versus buy versus outsource, leverage

Let's look at these one by one.

## 1. Product design

The product design decisions are customer-centric. Defining a customer business problem or a need, identifying customer segment and their buying behaviour, and ability and willingness to buy the product at a specific price, are decisions that are vital for designing the product and its features.

Before a car manufacturer designs a car, the team must have target customer and the price range in mind. The Tata Nano was designed for a customer who aspired to move from owning a 2-wheeler to owning a car. Thus, the design team did away with as many components that increase the cost, as possible. While the goal of pricing the Nano at below Rs. 1 lakh was not achieved, they were close. But for this key input on a target price, the car could have ended with components that cost Rs 3 lakhs. Thus, design cannot be independent from target price.

Additionally, the features that deliver expected customer benefits should also be divided into multiple categories, such as must have (basic), good to have (comfort) and nice to have (optional or luxury). The MoSCoW prioritisation method, an analytical technique used in management, business analysis, project management, and software development, divides customer benefits into four prioritisation categories (Must have, should have, could have, and Won't have). The "won't have" features are obviously left out, thus effectively having three possible variants.

Creating multiple product options that deliver different benefits helps capture a maximum number of customers within target segment, and also, maximise the profits.

## 2. Marketing

The four most important categories of marketing decisions are product, price, place and promotion. The "product" decisions involve choosing what to produce, how to design the product, and how to sell (discussed in the next paras).

The choice of place and promotion involves segmenting customers using criteria such as education levels, location, income levels, likes/ dislikes, industry and so on, assessing demand from those specific segments, choosing channels and messaging to reach out to and get those customers.

If you want to sell a product that requires customers to spend on an average Rs 100 or more per day per head, you can safely leave most poor and middle-class people out of your target segments. There may be a few exceptions to this rule, such as a private school education or mandatory medical treatment, which are examples of products (or services) that are essentials.

*"Effective pricing forms the backbone of a successful marketing strategy and holds the key to every organisation's long-term financial performance"*

***—Utpal Dholakia***

Protein supplements that are marketed and sold for fitness enthusiasts typically target customers who are in the higher middle class, luxurious and super-rich category. Their usage of channels, messaging, and pricing reflects this clearly. Traditional protein supplements that cost less than 20% of these (such as *sattu* or egg-whites) do not offer the same level of choice in flavour or ease of consumption as the branded protein supplements and are not marketed like branded protein supplements.

Thus, it is essential to understand the impact of positioning and pricing before estimating the demand for the product from the target customer segment.

## 3. Customer acquisition

The customer acquisition strategy includes identifying channels of customer acquisition, reach, the accuracy of targeting right customers, control on the channel performance, replicability, flexibility, conversion ratios and costs.

Having one's own sales team provides a higher level of accuracy in targeting the right customer segment, more control on performance and potentially better conversion ratio from prospect to customer. However, having its own sales team may pose challenges wider reach, replicability, flexibility and costs. Developing channel partners who are rewarded for performance may be a better option than having one's own sales team, especially in the geographies that are not core focus or a big enough market.

The cost of customer acquisition through each channel may be different. Therefore, optimising the spend on channels is key to lowering the cost of customer acquisition. While the price of a product may have to be maintained uniform across the channels, the discounts and offers can be used to offer the desired price to the customer who buys through a specific channel, where the cost of acquisition is lower.

## 4. Selling

While marketing focuses on building a brand, channels help draw the customer to the doorstep. In many cases, the salesperson is an inevitable last step in the customer acquisition process. The exception to this is online product selling. However, in the B2B market, salespersons (or "account managers") are involved in most transactions.

Even the companies that sell most technologically complex products with dozens of features attempt to create a sales playbook that focuses on select benefits and differentiators. The choice of which key benefits and differentiators to include in the paybook must be made carefully. Demonstrating how the product delivers the best value for money as compared to the competitors' product is almost always included in the playbook. However, each customer may prioritise their needs differently, and hence the measurement of value delivered may differ. In such a case, having modular products that provide different value at different price points makes a difference between a deal won and lost.

Product price also plays a crucial role in designing sales commissions, offers and discounts and sales pitch. The sales commissions are often tied to the discounts offered. Higher the discount provided to win the deal, lower the salesperson's commission. The salespersons, therefore, have an incentive to maximise the revenue for the organisation and structures the sales pitch accordingly.

## 5. Funding

Entrepreneurs are risk-takers by nature. Most businesses start with identification of customers that can be acquired in the short-term and the and products that can be sold. In most cases, the business plan and financial forecast is an afterthought. The preparation of a business plan is mostly undertaken when the entrepreneur wants to make a serious financial commitment or wants to raise fund from investors or lenders. While ideally, no business should be started without a proper business plan, in real life, this makes practical business sense.

A business plan involves identification of market opportunity for a specific product or a portfolio. The pricing of the product/s is essential criteria while identifying the addressable market and the target market. The customer acquisition plan is worked out based on these variables.

Thus, pricing is an essential input for preparing the financial model and forecasting for raising funds. Establishing the business viability as well as working out debt-raising and servicing capacity is critical for raising debt. Likewise, it is critical for establishing free cash flows and business valuation using relevant criteria such as free cash flows or revenue/profit multiples.

## 6. Investing

Most large corporates take investment decisions, such as for investing in assets, undertaking new projects or acquiring a business, after a thorough analysis of the proposal. Let's take an example of a company which is into manufacturing packaging boxes for electronic items like mobile phones, or quick-service restaurants like pizza chains.

The packaging needs of these products are complex. A package for mobile phone, an electronic item, has to look attractive, must preserve the item in different weather conditions, have space and compartments for properly arranging and storing components (such as headphone, warranty card, manual and the phone itself) and should provide basic safety from breakages from a fall. The package has to last for a few months in good condition since the customer may retain it. Likewise, a box in which pizza is carried to the customer for home delivery should not spill out the contents. In contrast, the delivery boy navigates the city traffic on his bike to fulfil 30-minute delivery commitment, quickly identify the contents inside into veg and non-veg, store accompaniments, and maintain the freshness and temperature of the pizza.

The manufacturer of these packaging boxes requires investment into specialised high-cost packaging manufacturing machines. The decision of investing in assets that carry such high costs won't be taken without a thorough analysis of the sales, profitability and cash flows. Estimating the improved pricing and sales from acquiring the new machine/s are the two most critical aspects on which such decision hinges.

The same considerations apply while undertaking an altogether new project or acquiring a business. A project or a business where the opportunities for improving prices is by and large not worth undertaking as a new investment.

## 7. Revenues

Every business activity is not geared towards earning revenue, though every entrepreneur would like it to be so. Typical examples of activities that do not directly generate revenues include customer education events, media presence of top management, contribution towards social projects, participation in industry member-only events, distributor or agent conferences, and so on.

The cost of such activities could be substantial. These costs must be budgeted from the revenues generated from goodwill and relationships created from these activities. Any such action that does not make an additional sale and help improve price should be ideally discontinued, except where legally mandated.

These expenses must be budgeted while pricing products because they impact net margins. The entrepreneur should create as many revenue earning products in the portfolio as possible. These different products can be designed and priced such that they create a successful funnel through which customer can experience value and move towards buying high-value products.

## 8. Profitability

It is relatively easier to simulate and measure the impact of pricing decisions on gross margins, as compared to the net margins unless you have a robust financial model of your business, which is updated with real-time data as the changes occur. That's the reason most companies are happy simulating and measuring the impact of price changes on the gross margin.

The gross margin calculations are done by calculating the costs that are directly attributable to producing and delivering a product. Any change in prices won't impact the behaviour of costs; hence the impact of change in price is direct and proportionate.

The indirect costs which are calculated to arrive at the net profit, do not change in the same proportion as the volume and price since they have a semi-fixed component.

Pricing decisions impact profitability at a gross level as well as the net level. We looked at this in Chapter 2 - Price = Growth + Profitability, by some running numbers in a hypothetical case.

## 9. Managing costs

The fundamental flaw with cost-plus pricing as a generic approach is that the market doesn't care about what expenses you incur while delivering products and services. If It were so, no business would make a loss. And innovation would cease because there is no incentive to produce products and services more efficiently.

Most customers would like to get all products and service free if that option is available. The power of 'free' is humongous. In his book "Predictably Irrational – The Hidden Forces That Shape Our Decisions", Dan Ariely explains how he concluded after several experiments that zero (price) is not just another discount. Zero is a different place. The difference between two cents and one cent is small. But the difference between one cent and zero is huge.

Thus, it is left to an entrepreneur that he manages the fixed, variable and semi-variable costs, to his advantage. The business should be structured to have as low a break-even point as possible, without sacrificing quality and customer satisfaction. The fact that many internationally well-known hospitality and restaurant brands do not own the real estate and most of the fixed assets at the point of customer service is a testimony to this fact.

## 10. Planning taxes

Most of the developed nations around the world have moved to value-added tax (VAT) regime, including India, which has moved to a Goods and Services Tax (GST) which provides credit for taxes paid on input items across the value chain, with a few exceptions.

The "output GST", i.e., the amount of tax charged on the goods and service sold in the value chain. Since the end consumer pays the highest price, the tax collected in effect is on that amount. In practice, most products are sold by the retailers to the end consumers at Maximum Retail Price (MRP) specified by the manufacturer or the brand owner. The MRP includes GST. Thus, the higher the MRP, the higher the GST. The discounts and offers can be reduced from the price to arrive at the GST payable.

Hence price-setting impacts the GST paid by the end consumer, and the revenue and profitability.

## 11. Cash flows

In the business-to-business market, extending credit to the customer is common-place. In a competitive scenario, at times, the period of credit extended makes a difference between a deal lost or won. However, credit extended to the customer increases the working capital tied up in business. Effectively you are extending your money to the customer for carrying on his business.

The credit also impacts the operating cash flows, since the ash realisation from revenues gets delayed. On the other hand, the cash required for running a business remains the same and keeps flowing out.

Providing cash discounts or rebates to the customer for cash purchases or early payment can improve the cash flows. However, these impact the profitability adversely, unless the discounts are calculated after taking the cost of capital into account. A cash discount provided to the customer at a rate less than or equal to the cost of capital will generally improve cash flows without denting the profitability. The recent changes in GST, effective April 1, 2020, are more favourable towards providing GST credit for cash rebates and discounts.

The cash budgets should be prepared after estimating the credit extended and the number of customers availing cash discount and paying against purchase or earlier.

## 12. Return on Investment (ROI)

The Return on Investment is influenced by profitability and investment made in the business. We looked at how profitability is affected by the pricing decisions. The investment decisions should also be evaluated in light of the pricing strategy.

The investment needed in the business is driven by the business model followed. E.g., a company that outsources most of its product manufacturing will need less investment in assets. A business which outsources its sales and marketing to partners who are paid based on results reduced cash outflow from sales and marketing activities to a point where close to the point where the revenue flows in, thus reducing the investment in working capital.

Taking debt or 'leveraging' capital reduces the investment made by the entrepreneur in business. Higher the leverage, lower the need for owners' capital. However, higher leverage also means higher debt servicing needs and higher risks. The leverage also impacts overall profitability. The ROI from owners' perspective can be improvised if the cost of debt is less than the profitability on the products.

Thus, key business decisions on building a business model, such as build versus buy versus outsource, and leverage are driven by the pricing strategy.

*"Pricing is the only element in the marketing mix that produces revenue; the other elements produce costs".*

***—Phillip Kotler***

# CHAPTER *Six*

## *Variables Involved in Pricing*

*"A good pricing decision is one that is made deliberately and thoughtfully, considers all relevant factors—costs, customer value, reference prices, and the value proposition, is based on the company's business philosophy & values, and is explained clearly to customers and to employees."*

***—Utpal Dholakia***

By now, you should be convinced that the pricing decisions are essential, and pricing strategy is an integral part of the business strategy.

Now that we want to be a price-setter, we should know which variables are involved in taking a pricing decision. These variables include:

1. Products and services
2. Business model
3. Target customer segment
4. Modularization/ versioning
5. Frequency of purchase
6. Perceived value
7. Alternatives and substitutes
8. Consumer trends
9. Branding power
10. Product lifecycle

Let's go through these ones by one.

## 1. Products and services

The nature of product or service itself may put certain limitations on the flexibility in pricing. The product or service characteristics that may influence this include:

(a) Production and delivery costs – Production and delivery costs affect the prices since every sale should recover these costs and additionally contribute towards the recovery of the fixed expenses.

(b) Ticket size – The nature of product dictates a specific price range within which most products are priced.

(c) Target audience - The product defines the target audience.

(d) Feasibility of differentiation - The product may or may not lend itself to creating a differentiated offering for different target segment and the needs.

(e) Government regulation – The pricing of some of the products, e.g., pharmaceutical products, is controlled by government regulations, thus leaving less scope for pricing flexibly.

(f) Physical versus virtual – some of the most valuable companies today deliver their services to the customers "virtually", e.g., Google, Facebook and Microsoft. Most of their costs are one-time costs and the same product is rolled out to the customers across the globe virtually. Thus, the cost of delivering to a new customer are near-zero. Companies that deliver physical products do not enjoy this advantage.

(g) Custom versus standardised – Some of the products need customisation to meet a specific customer's needs. This increases the costs in comparison to the standardised products.

(h) Necessity – comfort- luxury – The necessities have a bigger market as compared to luxury items. What is considered as a necessity in one market could be considered as comfort or luxury in another market.

It is important to note that these characteristics may also provide certain flexibility in pricing.

## 2. Business model

The business model chosen by the organisation has a direct impact on the investments made in fixed assets, and the variable costs incurred for producing each unit of product sold. The cost of producing every additional unit also called "marginal cost", has a significant impact on the price-setting exercise.

The decision to build major components of the products within the organisation usually means substantial investment in technology and infrastructure. Industries like automobiles and electronics manufacturing buy several parts needed to make (or assemble) the final product to leverage economies of scale that their vendors enjoy due to focus on producing those components. One of the key reasons for growth in outsourcing services providers is to move to a relatively asset-light model and maintain flexibility in tune with the demand.

Besides vendors, many organisations leverage a network of partners, who specialise in their areas and together help create a more significant go-to-market offering. This helps maintain focus on their own competency while tapping into more significant deals.

## 3. Target customer segment

Another factor that impacts pricing strategy is whether the products are sold to the businesses (B2B) or directly to the end consumers (B2C). Negotiation in price is common practice in the B2B market. In contrast, in the B2C market, usually, the end-consumer pays the MRP (maximum retail price), which is a mandatory disclosure in most countries. The end-consumer can still be offered additional benefits like exclusive offers (volume discounts), freebies (one-on-one free) etc.

Another segmentation of customers could be by their occupation, e.g., entrepreneurs, salaried professionals, retired people or students etc. Many off-the-shelf end-user IT product companies like Microsoft offer special prices to the students, to "catch them young" while their payment capacity is low.

Products targeted at women entrepreneurs can be priced higher relative to those that are aimed at homemakers, as long as value can be justified. The same product can be priced for international users at two to three times the price charged to Indian users, by providing extra features that don't cost much, by leveraging the higher purchasing power of the international customers.

## 4. Modularisation & Versioning

If a product can be modularised or created into different versions, the flexibility of pricing is much higher. Ability to create different versions of the same product to target different customer segments helps sell a larger number of products and provide the best value to the customer based on his needs and ability to pay.

Websites builders offer their products under categories such as personal, small business, enterprise and eCommerce. Additionally, they provide add-on features that can be bundled with the subscription to a specific category.

Enterprise solutions providers offer products under broad categories such as manufacturing, distribution, human resources, finance, and so on. Additionally, the pricing is based on a number of users.

Building products with the goal of modularising and versioning is the best strategy. The product design team should keep this as a goal.

## 5. Frequency of purchase

Items that are purchased frequently by the end-consumers must be priced such that they can afford those. Breakfast cereals, calcium tablets and biscuits are examples of such products. Their higher-priced versions include cereals with dates, raisins and cashews, calcium tablets with D-vitamin, and cookies or cream biscuits, respectively. These target consumers with higher spending power.

Items that are consumed rarely and those consumed one time can be relatively priced higher. Consumers generally average out the price by reminding themselves that these are needed one time or rarely.

## 6. Perceived value

As they say, the "beauty is in the eye of the beholder". In business parlance, we should translate it to mean that the customer is the best judge of value. As a general rule, the customer will be willing to pay higher for a product only if he perceives the product delivers higher value.

There are exceptions to this rule. Selling products and services that are a part of the discretionary spend of the target customer segment is always difficult as compared to non-discretionary or mandated spend. The perceived value delivered by products mandated by regulators may be less; however, the customer will spend the money. The discretionary spend decisions can always be postponed to a later date.

The perceived value keeps changing with the time and situation. If you are selling security systems such as CCTV cameras and intruder alarm systems, you will find it easier to conclude the sale in a neighbourhood where recently burglaries and thefts have occurred.

Customer perceived value is the total customer value minus total customer cost. Total customer value is the overall monetary benefit of the product, and the entire customer cost is the total fiscal costs the customer expects to incur in evaluating, obtaining, and using the product. Thus, the value perceived is impacted by the price charged. If you deliver high value at a higher price, the customer perceived value may be lower.

Since the laptops are easy to carry around compared to the desktops, the perceived benefit is higher. However, since the cost of owning a laptop over the long term, say, 5- year period may be higher, for heavy usage, customers still prefer a desktop.

## 7. Alternatives and substitutes

Availability of comparable options limits the scope for pricing the product higher. One of the ways of getting around this challenge is to articulate better the benefits that matter more to the customer and thus differentiate the product. This is usually a continuous exercise since the competitors also keep changing their messaging.

Availability of cheaper substitutes also limits the scope for pricing higher. In some cases, the alternatives could be priced very low. E.g., Home remedies cost much less than over-the-counter medicine. *Sattu* costs much less than protein supplements. However, it is relatively easy to articulate the product's value proposition vis-a-vis the substitutes.

## 8. Consumer trends

Consumer habits and preferences change rapidly. Moreover, these are now moulded by global trends. Products that target younger consumers are more exposed to the evolving patterns, since those consumers tend to copy the global trends rapidly.

Internet-enabled disintermediation is one such major trend that continues to gather strength from year to year. Ecommerce, instant credit from shadow-banks (non-banking finance companies), Software as a Service (SaaS), Platform as a Service (PaaS) and movies on demand are just a few examples of this trend. They have removed the need for intermediaries and consumers have developed a habit of consuming the products using these models.

Most hotels have moved to a buffet breakfast menu from *a la carte*. Telecom operators offer voice packages bundled with data packs. Brands that strictly sold office wear now sell jeans and casual clothes under "Friday dressing" theme. The pricing strategies must adapt to these trends.

## 9. Branding power

The difference between a branded product and unbranded product is that, in the latter case, you have to entirely rely on your expertise and judgement, and the advice of the seller. Other things being the same, the risk of buying an unbranded product is higher. You would typically get the unbranded product at a lower price, and it may also deliver the same level of benefits; however, there is a high level of uncertainty.

A brand assures the customer that the brand owner has taken efforts to ensure that the product meets the expectations of quality and performance that the brand represents. The large retailers and eCommerce players have invested in building 'store brands' that buy right quality products from established manufacturers, as "white labelled" products; i.e., without the manufacturer's brand.

Some of the successful companies have nurtured various brands and enjoy superior pricing power. One such example is Arvind Limited, a Lalbhai group company, that owns leading clothing brands like Newport, Ruf & Tuf, Excalibur, besides marketing other brands in India. Aditya Birla group's Madura Garments owns brands like Allen Solly, Peter England and Louis Phillippe. Volkswagen Group of Germany owns brands like Audi, Bentley, Bugatti, Lamborghini, Porsche, SEAT, Škoda and the flagship Volkswagen marques. These companies enjoy pricing power which is derived from the brand's potential.

## 10. Product lifecycle

The pricing strategy doesn't remain the same throughout the product's lifecycle. Some of the strategies that the product may follow during various stages of its lifecycle are given below by way of example.

| ***Stage of Product Life- Cycle*** | ***Pricing Strategies*** | ***Business Goal*** |
|---|---|---|
| Research and Development | Referrals, Free Trial | Get customer validation of the product |
| Growth | Penetration | Grow customer base and revenue |
| Maturity | Volume, Marginal | Use economies of scale to capture market share |
| Decline | Skimming | Leverage competitive position for high profitability |

These strategies are discussed in the later chapters.

*"You can determine the strength of a business over time by the amount of agony they go through in raising prices."*

***—Warren Buffett***

# CHAPTER *Seven*

## *Overview of Pricing Strategies*

*"Pricing is the moment of truth – all of marketing strategy comes to focus on the pricing decision."*

***—Raymond Corey***

Product and services pricing, as a strategy, has evolved considerably over the last few decades. We can broadly divide these strategies into a few categories, as follows:

1. Traditional
2. Sales driven
3. Modern
4. Risk- reward based
5. Innovative

These categories are neither carved in stone nor are they 'exclusive'. That is, you may want to put a strategy that I have classified under sales-driven strategy as a modern or innovative strategy. Likewise, a strategy categorised as sales-driven may also fall into a category of 'modern' strategy at the same time. This is simply how I have categorised for the sake of discussion in this book.

The best approach in real-life would be to understand these strategies, how they are used, their advantages and limitations, and then customise and use the ones that you find workable, in the specific context of your business. You may also follow different strategies in isolation or combination in various lines of business or different geographies.

Let's look at these categories one by one. In the later chapters, we delve into each of these strategies.

## Basis of classification

The broad categorisation of these strategies under 4 is made using the following criteria.

| *Criteria* | *Traditional* | *Sales driven* | *Modern* | *Risk-Reward* | *Innovative* |
|---|---|---|---|---|---|
| Length of use | Centuries | Decades | Decades | Recent | Recent |
| Cross-industry usage | High | High | Medium | Medium | Low |
| Creativity and innovation | Low | Low | Medium | Medium | High |
| Complexity of analysis | Low | Medium | Medium | Medium | High |
| Level of differentiation | Low | Low | Medium | Medium | High |
| Deployment of technology | Low | Low | High | Low | High |
| Regulatory complexity | Low | Medium | High | High | High |

## Pricing Strategies

The strategies listed below are covered in the chapters that follow.

1. **Traditional strategies**
    1. Cost-plus
    2. Follow the leader

3. Penetration pricing
4. Effort based
5. Fixed-price

**2. Sales driven strategies**

6. Introductory
7. Benchmarking
8. Price to Win
9. Volume pricing
10. Auction pricing
11. Government pricing
12. Special Offers
13. Guerrilla pricing

**3. Modern strategies**

14. Segment pricing
15. Referral Discounts
16. Add-ons
17. Marginal pricing
18. Geographical
19. White label pricing
20. Bundle pricing
21. Value-based

4. **Risk-Rewards based**
    22. One-time license
    23. License & Renewal
    24. Free trial
    25. ROI based
    26. Pricing product co-creation
    27. Pricing for product validation
    28. Money-Back Guarantees
    29. Transaction based
    30. Goals- linked
5. **Innovative strategies**
    31. Customer as a data
    32. Click & Mortar
    33. Pricing a niche
    34. Modular vs enterprise
    35. Choice/ Anchoring/ Decoy
    36. Yes/ No pricing
    37. Dynamic
    38. Funnel pricing / Zero price
    39. Pre-selling
    40. Pay – as – you – wish

41. Cannibalisation/ Price skimming
42. Freemium/ Subscription (SaaS/PaaS)

*"Never, ever suggest they don't have to pay you. What they pay for, they'll value. What they get for free, they'll take for granted, and then demand as a right. Hold them up for all the market will bear."*

***—Lois McMaster Bujold***

# CHAPTER *Eight*

# *Traditional Pricing Strategies*

*"The bitterness of poor quality remains long after the sweetness of low price is forgotten."*

***—Benjamin Franklin***

We classified pricing strategies into 5 broad categories - traditional, sales-driven, modern, risk-reward based and innovative. The "traditional" strategies are in use for centuries across industries. Let's look at the advantages and limitations of following traditional pricing strategies.

## Advantages of traditional pricing strategies

1. Intuitive and make a strong business sense at an early stage
2. Simple to understand and explain
3. At times easy to implement
4. The relative ease of gathering required data
5. Do not need complex analysis
6. Easy to measure success and improvise
7. Needs low creativity and innovation

## Limitations of traditional pricing strategies

1. "Me too" strategies- easy to replicate
2. Don't factor in different customer segments

3. No competitive advantage
4. Don't align with customer goals
5. Full/ substantial risk is with the customer
6. Do not leverage advances in data analytics
7. Difficult to leverage digital channels

## Traditional pricing strategies

Some of the key conventional pricing strategies include

1. Cost-plus
2. Follow-the-leader
3. Penetration pricing
4. Effort based
5. Fixed-price

Let's look at the above traditional pricing strategies one by one.

## 1. Cost-plus

One of the easiest ways to price a product is to link it to the costs of production and delivery. Find out the costs involved in producing the product, estimate fixed costs such as rent, salaries of support staff, and management overheads, and add expected profit on top of that.

The cost-plus contracts were popular with large public sector undertakings and with governments. The customer enjoys the satisfaction of knowing how much profit the vendor makes. The negotiation focuses on the percentage mark-up that vendor should charge. The bureaucrats who decide on the vendor find it easy to justify the decision by comparing the mark-up on comparable costs.

Cost-plus contracts pass on the entire risk of an increase in material and labour costs, variance on account of any inefficiencies, and the cost of fixing defects to the customer. The vendor has no incentive to be efficient and control costs. If the costs go up, the percentage mark-up being the same, the vendor makes more profit in absolute terms. Procuring material at higher costs as well as loading more overhead costs works in favour of the vendor. The customer is likely to suffer by taking on all the risks in return for the satisfaction of controlling the profit made by the vendor.

| ***Component*** | ***Cost-Plus Contract Terms*** | ***Expected Scenario Rs*** | ***Actual Scenario 1 Rs*** | ***Actual Scenario 2 Rs*** |
|---|---|---|---|---|
| Material | 50.00% | 50000 | 40000 | 60000 |
| Labour | 35.00% | 35000 | 30000 | 40000 |
| Overhead | 15.00% | 15000 | 15000 | 10000 |
| Total cost | 100.00% | 100000 | 85000 | 110000 |
| Profit margin | 20.00% | 20000 | 17000 | 22000 |
| Contract value | 120.00% | 120000 | 102000 | 132000 |

An example of how cost-plus contracts work is given above. The project is expected to cost Rs 1,20,000 to the customer, as per contract terms and estimation (estimated scenario).

If the vendor demonstrates efficiencies in using material and labour (actual scenario 1), the customer benefits, since the project costs Rs. 1,02,000, a saving of 15% from the estimation. The vendor, however, ends up with a lower profit of Rs. 17,000, against an estimated Rs. 20,000. Thus, the vendor is penalised for efficient execution!

If the vendor is inefficient in using material and labour (actual scenario 2), the customer suffers, since the project costs Rs. 1,32,000, an escalation of 10% from the estimation. The vendor, however, ends up with a higher profit of Rs. 22,000, against an estimated Rs. 20,000. Thus, the vendor is rewarded for inefficient execution!

These situations can be awarded by incorporating terms in the contract that provide additional incentive to the vendor for efficiencies and penalising he vendor for inefficiencies.

In India, maintenance of cost records and audit of those records is mandatory for companies in specific industries which fulfil additional criteria of size. This is a hang-over from the socialist days and continues. The strategy is still popular where the customer is a monopoly in a particular sector (e.g., defence departments), and award contracts for building products specific to their unique requirements. Since the requirements are unique, the vendor is also assured that investments towards developing unique products, which is otherwise a loss, can be fully recovered from the contract itself. Also, if the customer demands additional deliverables, the vendor can include those and pass on the costs to the customer, thus maintaining flexibility in meeting customer needs.

Cost-plus pricing is the most avoidable strategy and is not popular today. It survives in the form of cost-plus percentage-based "transfer pricing" mechanism, where entities within the business group deliver products and services to another entity within the same group. Tax laws in India (and many other countries) require an "audit" or "certification" of transfer pricing contracts and transactions between related entities, to ensure there is no tax evasion.

Cost-plus strategy can be used in combination with marginal pricing or white-label pricing strategies that are explained elsewhere, to maintain profitability to a certain level, while generating economies of scale.

***Cost-plus pricing – Checklist:***

| | |
|---|---|
| 1 | Does the deal involve procurement of a product or service, or delivering a project, that has unique requirements that are not relevant for most other customers? |
| 2 | Does the customer have the need as well as the expertise to monitor the costs incurred by the vendor with a reasonable degree of accuracy? |

| | |
|---|---|
| 3 | Is it possible to define incentives for better performance and levy penalties for unsatisfactory performance, using objective, measurable criteria? |
| 4 | Is the scope of the contract clearly defined, to identify the possible reasons for cost escalations? |

## 2. Follow-the-leader

It is not unusual for an industry leader to set the standards that most other players in the industry follow. Simultaneous usage of 'Control' and 'C' keys (Ctrl+C) for text copying, and 'Control' and 'V' keys (Ctrl+V) for text pasting was chosen by designers at Xerox. Later Microsoft and others popularised it so much that it has become a de-facto industry standard for this function.

The industry leaders also define a standard for product design, packaging, measure and price. The advantages of following the leader are apparent. All the hard work of explaining the concept and convincing about the benefits is already done. The benchmark of price is set in the buyer's mind. If the product looks similar, works similar and delivers similar benefits, selling is relatively easy.

The industry leader usually makes substantially high investments in creating the market for the product. The other players don't have to incur those costs. However, they have the flexibility of pricing their product around the price charged by the leader. When foreign brands like Starbucks and Pizza Hut enter, their local Indian competitors can benefit by increasing the price closer to the levels of these MNC players.

However, it must also be kept in mind that the customers' expectations are also set higher by the leader. Unless the customer gets the same benefits and experience, he won't quickly shell out a similar price. In a large and diversified market like India, this provides both challenges and opportunities for entrepreneurs. If the leader has superior technology and has built a large base that offer economies of scale, it is complicated as well as risky to use the follow-the-leader strategy. You may have to match the deep pockets and risk appetite of the leader.

In some cases, aligning the pricing strategy with that of the industry leader may be perceived as a case of price collusion or "fixing" prices, in sync with the leader, by the industry regulators. Such practices are prohibited because they reduce the competition ad lead to monopolistic choices for the consumers.

With the emergence and popularity of price comparison engines, the large retailers and eCommerce players frequently change their prices to match or better the competitor's prices. The websites that compare the bank's lending rates and premiums for insurance force the players to review their strategies to as closely match the industry leader's pricing as is practical.

Follow- the- leader pricing should not be confused with "leader pricing" or "loss-leader" strategy policy used by some of the businesses to attract customers by selling products below cost, and make a profit from cross-sell and up-sell of other products that generate profits.

***Follow- the- leader pricing – Checklist:***

| | |
|---|---|
| 1 | Is the demand for the product price-elastic? |
| 2 | Is the feasibility of setting the prices based on the pricing strategy of the leader worked out? |
| 3 | Does pricing the product in line with the leader's prices make it easier to sell? |
| 4 | Have you incorporated the possible changes in the leader's pricing strategy in response to your pricing? |
| 5 | Are you able to meet the customer's expectations such that they would find the price to value derived from your product better than the leader's |

## 3. Penetration pricing

Penetration pricing, as the name suggests, is used to penetrate a market, using a low price as the differentiator. The goal is to sell as much volume to as many customers as possible and generate a buzz that would help sustain the high rate of growth. This is a strategy used at the stage where the product is being introduced in the market. A company may use this strategy for a well- established product while entering a new market, where the product is unknown.

Restaurants price the food lower for the first few months of the launch, to attract the customers and raise the prices slowly to the desired level in two or three revisions. Restaurants that list on the food aggregator platforms initially price the food lower than menu prices for dining-in. Consultants sign-up the initial customers at a lower price point than usual to prove their capabilities, and later use these case studies to market their expertise.

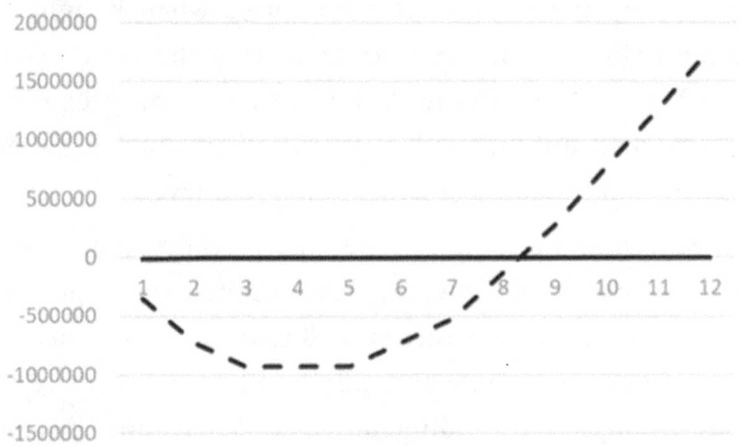


The above graph depicts results of penetration pricing strategy using a hypothetical case, where the product is sold at a loss for first 3 months from launch, at no profit-no loss for the next 3months. Subsequently, the price is steadily increased by small percentages over the next 6 months. If the volume of sales in the first 6 months of penetration pricing is sustained, the cumulative result would be a profit over 12 months.

Penetration pricing can be used to retain the customers in the face of a new competitor. The incumbent may drop the price temporarily to maintain the customer in the face of the lower price offered by the new entrant. Prolonged usage of such strategy to outsmart and outmanoeuvre the competition is also called "guerrilla" pricing strategy. In both cases, the lower prices can't be a long-term sustainable strategy, because of the low profitability.

Penetration pricing can be used more effectively by offering the product at a low price when bought in combination with another product from the same seller. Another way of offering a low price, is by providing volume discount for small quantities than usual, e.g., one unit free on purchase of two, at the retail level.

Penetration pricing is frequently used by product and services providers. However, it has limited use in pricing projects, since their nature is such that the next project is usually of considerable variation and hence mostly again goes through the bidding process. Penetration pricing works because the customer's risk of money is reduced; however, the seller has a risk of not being able to sell further or being able to increase the price later. Once the product gains the acceptance of the customers, the prices are slowly restored to the usual level in a step by step increments.

'Price skimming', another strategy explained elsewhere, is opposite of the penetration pricing strategy, if used during the initial launch of the product. Penetration pricing strategy may be used by a business over the long term to attract customers and cross-sell and up-sell other products that generate high profits; in that case, this strategy is also called loss-leader strategy.

***Penetration pricing – Checklist:***

| | |
|---|---|
| 1 | Is low price a key differentiator for your product that would provide an incentive for the customer to try your product over the established ones? |
| 2 | Do the expected sales volumes from quicker customer acquisition and subsequent purchases justify the lower margins on the initial sales? |
| 3 | Is it possible to raise the product prices subsequently without causing significant customer attrition? |
| 4 | What is the likelihood of the established players responding with dropping the prices and triggering a price war? |

## 4. Effort based

Effort based pricing, also known as timesheet- based pricing, has been a standard practice in some of the industries. The lawyers have been billing the clients based on hours spent on the case. Accountants bill to the clients based on the timesheet. IT Services (ITS) and IT-enabled Services (ITeS) companies in India developed a global leadership position while billing the customers on efforts basis. Even while bidding for projects, effort-based pricing is used for the services component, in most cases.

Effort based price is easy to calculate. Lawyers log the timesheet, the billing clerks total up the time spent for each client's work, multiply the time by the rate agreed for the lawyer's profile, and send the bill to the client. The client pays the bill as long he trusts the firm. The more a lawyer works, more he bills and more the firm earns. Since the lawyer is working for the client, the client assumes that he will gain from the expertise accordingly. Several timesheets- based billing software applications are available in the market, many of them for free or a very low price. These applications provide time tracking, reporting and invoicing capabilities, which makes timesheet- based billing easier today, than earlier.

The effort-based pricing passes on all the risks of performance to the client. If the lawyer or accountant in the firm is inefficient and therefore takes more time to complete the work, or provides wrong advice after preparing for the case, the client ends up paying for the efforts undertaken, nevertheless. There is neither an incentive for being efficient nor a linkage with performance. The customers pay for the results, and not for the efforts. Hence time sheet based- billing still exists where the customers exercise control over the performance, e.g., billing by the professionals who work with the customer on contract under the client's supervision.

Though many advisers have moved away from pure effort- based billing, and quote fixed fees for a consulting assignment, in most cases, the underlying basis continues to be the efforts required to execute the task. The customers insist on linking the billing to the milestones that are connected to the deliverables that the customers expect.

***Effort based pricing – Checklist:***

| | |
|---|---|
| 1 | Is effort- based billing a common pricing strategy in your industry? |
| 2 | Does effort- based billing provide you with an opportunity to manage your costs and profitability? |
| 3 | Are you able to allocate tasks to staff based on roles and align the deliverables such that the margins are maintained? |
| 4 | Do you have a system in place for logging, approving, tracking and invoicing the efforts to the customers? |

## 5. Fixed-price

Since the effort- based pricing passes on the entire risk to the client, some of the clients started demanding a fixed price for services. If you pick up an annual report of any Indian IT company from the last decade, you will find Directors Report mentioning how the company is striving to move to a fixed price for projects. The ratio of client projects executed on time and material basis (efforts basis) to the projects completed on a fixed price basis is disclosed in the annual report.

A well-drafted fixed price contract must ensure that the responsibility for performance is well-defined for both the parties. There must be clarity on the problem being solved, proposed solution deliverables and the acceptance criteria. The vendor would also like to add a buffer or contingency to cover for managing risks that are not foreseen while signing the contract. Documenting the assumptions, roles and responsibilities of each party, responsibility of the third-parties, dependencies, schedule and billing is critical for a fixed price contract.

The fixed price, however, requires that the scope is fixed. Whenever presented with a scope document, clients are, in many cases, sign-off on the document. This makes it difficult for the vendor to quote a fixed price. Therefore, a hybrid pricing strategy, "time and material with cap" or "capped T&M" evolved. The vendor has some flexibility to negotiate beyond initial price; however, the increase is capped to a certain amount. This hybrid pricing strategy protects the interest of the vendor while capping the money- risk for the client.

The fixed-price contract is not truly an outcome-based pricing contract. The outcomes defined in the fixed price contract usually cover the contract's deliverables, but do not cross into the results that the customer expects by undertaking the project.

***Fixed price – Checklist:***

| | |
|---|---|
| 1 | Are the scope and deliverables clearly defined? |
| 2 | Are the performance expectations, roles and responsibilities of all the parties to a contract, as well as of the critical third parties, clearly defined? |
| 3 | Are you able to manage the deliverables within time and budget, given the contingency buffer provided for in the contract? |

## Comparison of Traditional Strategies

The table below compares various traditional strategies.

| *Criteria* | *Cost-Plus* | *Follow-The-Leader* | *Penetration* | *Effort based* | *Fixed-Price* |
|---|---|---|---|---|---|
| Risk for vendor | Low | Medium | High | Low | Medium |
| Risk for customer | High | Low | Low | High | Medium |
| Usage in Projects pricing | High | Low | Low | Services | Projects |
| Usage in Products pricing | Medium | High | High | Low | Low |
| Usage in Services pricing | Low | High | High | High | Medium |
| Usage in the B2B market | Medium | Medium | Medium | Medium | Medium |
| Usage in the B2C market | Low | High | High | Low | Low |

*"Consumers rarely respond to the lower prices enough to offset lower margins."*

***—Kurt Jetta***

# CHAPTER *Nine*

## *Sales-Driven Pricing Strategies*

*"There is no point in matching a competitor if the nearest store is 50 miles away."*

***—Graeme McVie***

We classified pricing strategies into 5 broad categories - traditional, sales-driven, modern, risk-reward based and innovative. The "sales-driven" strategies are viral and effective. Let's look at the advantages and limitations of following sales-driven pricing strategies.

## Advantages of sales-driven pricing strategies

1. Motivates sales team
2. Improves win/ loss ratio
3. More deals, more revenue
4. Growth focused
5. Quantifying results is easier

## Limitations of sales-driven pricing strategies

1. Disconnect with value delivered
2. Difficult to roll back
3. Tend to be permanent
4. No incentive for creativity & innovation
5. May invite guerrilla pricing tactics

## Sales-driven pricing strategies

Some of the critical sales-driven pricing strategies include

1. Introductory
2. Benchmarked pricing
3. Price to Win
4. Volume pricing
5. Auction pricing
6. Government pricing
7. Special Offers
8. Guerrilla pricing

Let's look at the sales-driven pricing strategies, one by one.

## 1. Introductory

"Introductory" offers are commonplace in household items. Usually, when an established brand expands into a related category or adds a new product within an established category, it wants to encash the goodwill of the existing customers. These customers have been so far purchasing the newly introduced product from other sellers. Most likely, they would also be happy with the current purchase. In this case, they need a 'nudge' to move to your newly introduced product.

The 'nudge' is best provided by introducing the new product under the umbrella brand that the customers are familiar with. Ideally, the product design and packaging should also follow the design and packaging for the existing products, so that the customer establish connect with the product. The price point may be, however, different, this being a new product.

One more way of incentivising the customers to experiment with the new product is to bundle it with a closely related product, for example, a toothbrush with toothpaste, shaving gel with shaving bled, and so on. A special offer where a higher discount is given for buying those two items together makes a direct comparison to the other brand's product difficult.

If the marginal cost of producing and delivering an additional unit of the new product is negligible, introducing the new product free, or with a trial free period, can get more customers to try the product. This helps get early user feedback and improvise the product. Favourable user feedback and testimonials are useful when the introductory offer period is over, and the product is pitched at the usual price.

It is key that the customers are aware of the introductory offer and price as a one-time and limited period offer. It must be firmly planted in the minds of the customer that the price is expected to be raised subsequently. If they are happy with the value obtained vis-a-vis the post-introductory period price, they will buy the product. While making introductory price offers to customers, care should be taken to ensure that the existing customers are not unhappy that they do not get the same offer.

Introductory pricing strategy looks deceptively close to penetration pricing strategy. The key differences between these two strategies is that

a. The initial pricing offers can be made to a select customer/s based on specific criteria, e.g., membership of a network or a business, or previous purchases of products from the same seller, and

b. Introductory pricing offer communicates to the customer that the special pricing is not a long-term strategy and that they should expect the price to increase.

***Introductory pricing – Checklist:***

| | |
|---|---|
| 1 | Have you defined a criterion to identify the customers to whom the introductory pricing offers should be made? |
| 2 | Are you communicating to the customers that the price offered is an introductory price and that they should expect the price to rise? |
| 3 | Are you confident in generating business from the customers once the product is provided at the usual price? |

## 2. Benchmarked pricing

Benchmarking involves identifying a standard that one wants to be measured against and then evaluating against that standard. The process of Benchmarking consists of defining what you want to benchmark, identifying the standard, analysing vis-à-vis the standard, and determine where you stand.

A product or a process can be benchmarked against a standard specified for the product or process. Alternatively, you can identify relevant products or methods used in practice, and benchmark against those. While the product design would like to benchmark against a standard first, the marketing team may want to benchmark against the competing product.

Benchmarking against competing product would involve analysing the products pricing, offers, sales strategy and value delivered. This can be used for the training sales team so that they handle customer objections and demonstrate the advantages vis-à-vis the competing product.

Benchmark pricing is commonly used in the commodities markets where the most significant producer or the market leader sets the price, which acts as a reference to the other players. This strategy works well in the commodities markets since commodity prices usually move within most countries in tandem with international prices.

Benchmarked pricing, on the face of it, is similar to the traditional "follow-the-leader" pricing strategy. However, in this case, you choose to benchmark against your closest competitor rather than the market leader, because those are the ones that your customer evaluates you against. Benchmarked pricing strategy may be applied selectively in some markets. In contrast, follow-the – leader pricing strategy generally assumes that pricing regarding the market leader will be used universally.

Before using benchmarked pricing strategy, the impact of the movement in the benchmark on profitability should be analysed. The competitor may be able to sustain those prices because of economies of scale or deep pockets; whether this is strategy sustainable has to be therefore explored in advance.

***Benchmarked pricing – Checklist:***

| | |
|---|---|
| 1 | Have you identified the competitor against whose product you want to benchmark your product pricing? |
| 2 | Have you identified the customer segment and market where the benchmarked pricing strategy will be followed? |
| 3 | Have you analysed the potential risks in following the benchmarked pricing strategy? |

## 3. Price to Win

In theory, price to win is more of a sales tactic, than a strategy. However, in many business-to-business deals, this tactic is so frequently followed by the salespersons, that it appears more like a strategy. Successful companies develop a process to manage deal pricing, to ensure a high win/ loss ratio and get the right results.

Typically, when the vendors compete in a bid, there are steps involved in the process, like submitting a Request for Information (RFI), and later qualifying through the preliminary review of the Request for Proposal (RFP). Once shortlisted, the select vendors compete with each other. The scope delivered, the risks involved and price and the most important criteria at this final stage of selection.

It is not unusual for the customer to indicate to the vendors the price that they are looking at to make a quick decision. Usually, this is expressed in terms of a budgetary constraint. Also, the customer may provide an opportunity to re-price the bid by de-scoping some items that they can cover on their own.

At this stage, most salespersons come up with a price that they believe can win the deal. Having satisfied the other criteria specified by the customer, and being shortlisted within a select few, they think that the change in price will seal the deal. Descoping some items may achieve this. Alternatively, the buffer for contingencies may be sacrificed by trying to put restrictions on change in scope.

Price to won strategy doesn't imply win-at-any-cost. The vendor must follow their guidelines for the level of acceptable risk, profitability and linkage to the customer lifetime value. If not, the winner may end up with a "winner's curse", a term used in auction pricing. That is, the bid may be won on terms that don't make commercial sense.

Price to win strategy is frequently followed in the last stages of the bidding process for government contracts. In large projects' bidding process, once the number of bidders is down to 2 or 3, from initial large quantities, it is possible to suggest solution alternatives to the customer. This includes de-scoping, changes in design, suggesting direct contract of the customer with the third-party vendors, changes in warranty and support terms, and so on. This provides scope for price changes. The 'cost- plus' pricing strategy can also be proposed as an alternative for those parts of the bid that carry a very high risk of escalation in costs.

Successful implementation of price to win strategy needs an in-depth knowledge of the competition. Having insights into the customer's organisation as well as hiring outside experts with intimate knowledge of the competition are helpful in this situation.

***Price to win – Checklist:***

| | |
|---|---|
| 1 | Are you in a situation where competitive pricing of the deal is imperative for winning the deal? |
| 2 | Have you exhausted all the other options of cutting down costs, optimising delivery and reducing the risk? |
| 3 | Do you understand the competition very well? |
| 4 | Do you have insights into the customer organisation? |

## 4. Volume pricing

A product's usual sales order quantity is within a specific range, depending on the channel through which the sales are made. The quantity ordered by a wholesaler is higher than the quantity ordered by the retailer. The end consumer usually buys in the lowest range for the quantity.

To attract higher sales volume and advance the purchase decisions, offering volume discounts is a customary practice. It is possible to sell a dozen ball-point pens to the customer, by offering those at Rs 5 per pen against a price of Rs 6 per pen for a lesser quantity. Determining the usual quantum of purchase and the maximum quantity that the customer will be enticed into buying by offering a lower price is key to this strategy.

A modified version of this strategy is deployed by the eCommerce portals by displaying the "frequently bought together" pair of items alongside the item being reviewed by the customer. An extra discount on the two items if bought together is an incentive for the customer to buy two things instead of one which he is contemplating to buy. Yet another version is "free shipping if the order exceeds" a certain amount. The eCommerce players are leveraging the volume pricing strategy innovatively since the cost of selling additional item is nearly zero, and the cost of delivery goes down with the economies of scale.

Volume pricing is an excellent way of separating different types of customers. A commercial user of printing and stationery items buys those in more significant quantity as compared to one who plans to use these at home. Offering a volume discount for larger quantity helps sell larger quantity at one go and leverage economies of scale in distribution.

The volume pricing strategy reduces the profitability on the whole deal if the customer agrees to buy the required volume that qualifies for the lower price. If the volume discounts are structured using a 'tiered pricing' approach, the profitability on the lower tiers is maintained higher. Thus, overall profitability is higher compared to the vanilla volume pricing deal.

An example below illustrates the difference in everyday vanilla volume pricing and tiered pricing.

| Deal Volume | Volume Pricing | | | Tiered Pricing | | |
|---|---|---|---|---|---|---|
| | Actual Sale Qty | Price | Sale Value | Actual Sale Qty | Tiered Price | Sale Value |
| 01-25 | 25 | 10.00 | 250.00 | 25 | 10.00 | 250.00 |
| 26-50 | 50 | 10.00 | 500.00 | 50 | 9.50 | 487.50 |
| 51-75 | 75 | 10.00 | 750.00 | 75 | 9.00 | 712.50 |
| 75+ | 100 | 8.00 | 800.00 | 100 | 8.00 | 912.50 |

The tiered pricing approach is less profitable until the sales quantity of 75; however, it protects profitability better if the quantity exceeds 75. It also encourages the customer to gradually move into purchasing higher quantity, rather than risk excess inventory and risk of obsolescence and wear and tear. The reduction for buying larger volumes have to be worked out after considering the reduced cost of customer acquisition, reduced cost of carrying inventory, economies of delivery and reduced cost of customer service.

Large buyers frequently ask for volume discounts from the vendors, where they expect these discounts to be built into the price. If the vendor agrees to the discount and starts supplying at lower rates upfront, he risks profitability, if the promised volumes do not come through. One way of structuring volume discount in these cases is the tiered approach as illustrated above *on cumulative basis*, so that the discounts are linked to the customer fulfilling his promise of volume purchases.

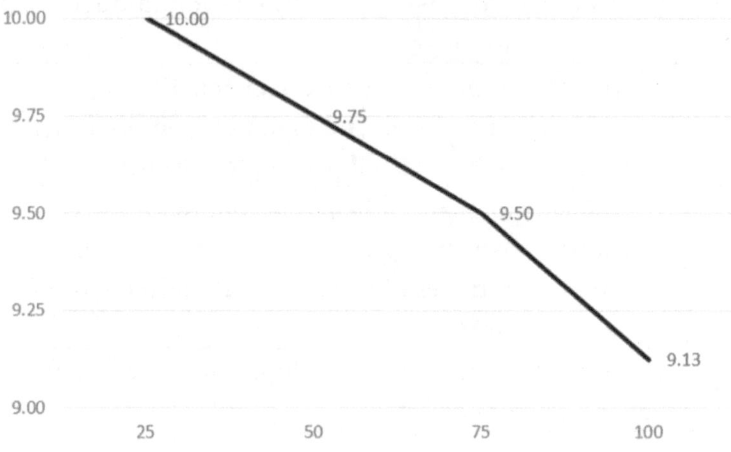


The customer will get his desired price of Rs. 9.13 per unit only if he buys a *cumulative total* of 100 items, which he had promised.

Bulk buying from the customers, if against credit, leads to higher working capital requirement for carrying debtors, as well as higher risk of default (credit risk). These should be weighed in a while agreeing to the volume pricing / tiered pricing of the deal.

***Volume pricing – Checklist:***

| | |
|---|---|
| 1 | Are you aware of the consumption pattern, frequency of purchase and volume of purchases across your customer segments? |
| 2 | Will volume pricing / tiered pricing lead to additional purchases by the customer, or the customer would have bought those quantities anyway? |
| 3 | Does your volume / tiered pricing strategy incentivise the customers to make the additional commitment that leads to savings for you? |
| 4 | Are you able to model the financial benefits from a large volume of the deal, and maintain your margins after giving volume/ tiered pricing to the customer? |
| 5 | Are you able to quantify benefits from reduced cost of customer acquisition, reduced cost of carrying inventory, economies of delivery and reduced cost of customer service? |
| 6 | Are you able to handle high volume and potential of higher risk from credit? |

## 5. Auction pricing

Auctions are popular in disposing off assets in a transparent way. Arts galleries regularly conduct auctions for selling arts artefacts. Banks auction off properties possessed from the defaulters. Tax authorities sell – off properties attached to recover tax dues. Auctions are more popular for products that are non-standardised and therefore need a transparent, competitive bidding environment to discover the price.

Options could involve open bids, where participants know what the other participants are bidding, or sealed bids, where the bids submitted remain secret from other participants.

Reserve Bank of India and its counterparts conduct the auction of treasury bills and government securities as per calendar published in advance at the beginning of the financial year. Clearing Houses do auctions to procure securities on behalf of the brokers and dealers who fail to deliver their securities for settlement at the end of the trading cycle.

The auctioneer sets a floor price below which the bids are not accepted. They also set the minimum bid increment (MBI), i.e., a minimum amount that a new bid must exceed the current price, for it to be accepted as a valid bid. This is done after careful analysis of potential prize that the auctioned item is likely to fetch. The items in the catalogue are carefully evaluated by the expert valuers in advance to ensure that the best price is obtained on the day of the auction. The auctioneer's performance is regularly evaluated against a benchmark set by the peers.

Auctions are one of the ways of price discovery. The bids submitted by the securities dealers helps the RBI discover the prices at which the dealers are willing to buy and the quantities they want to buy at that price. Accordingly, the RBI sets a cut-off at which the securities are allotted to the bidders.

The flowers in Amsterdam, Holland, the biggest market for flowers internationally, are sold using 'Dutch auction' strategy, where the seller starts with a higher price, and keeps lowering the price, till the flowers are sold-out. The buyers are thus engaged in 'reverse bidding' instead of the usual bidding higher to buy the product.

The eCommerce players extended the concept of auctions to the dealings between consumers (consumer to consumer – C2C), by developing the e-auction model. The bidding in e-auction marketplace takes place electronically. The seller fixes the reserve price below which the bids are not entertained. The concept has become famous for relatively low value used and new items like household items and electronic items. The concept has now been extended to other markets like used car markets, which has a higher ticket size, where the seller is using brick-and-mortar model to sell the used cars.

The e-auction marketplaces like Shopify and eBay have evolved to provide various auction pricing strategies, such as

- Regular (forward) auction – where buyers compete with each other, with bids moving up from the reserve price
- Reverse auction – where sellers compete with each other, with bids moving down from a higher price
- English auction – where sellers set the minimum bidding amount from where buyers have to start bidding

- Dutch auction – where buyers set the minimum bidding amount from which the bids begin
- Private auction – where only selected buyers are invited to participate and
- Penny auction – where buyers are asked to put up an upfront deposit to qualify to bid

Bidding at auction requires specialised knowledge and skills. Bidders who bid very aggressively to win the bid in an auction, may end up with a "winner's curse". That is, they may end up winning a bid at a price which is way out of the market, and hence a decision which leads to a loss. Astute bidders have a pre-defined upper limit for the price that they are willing to offer and continuously monitor auction to ensure they don't end up being cursed winners.

***Auction pricing – Checklist:***

| | |
|---|---|
| 1 | Is your product a non-standardised one, where customers find it difficult to decide whether they should buy at that price? |
| 2 | Is it worth undergoing the listing and bidding process for discovering the price of your product? |
| 3 | Have you calculated risks from the bids not working as desired? |
| 4 | Will your product create enough interest such that a fairly large number of bidders bid for the product for robust price discovery? |
| 5 | Are you able to decide which type of auction works better for your production, e.g., regular (forward) auction versus reverse auction? |

## 6. Government pricing

Governments (central and state), municipalities, defence, and public sector undertakings are one of the biggest customers in most economies. Successful privatisation has reduced the size of government in a few economies; still, the government continues to be a valuable customer with huge buying power.

Since the bureaucrats run the government procurement process, they are generally reluctant to take the decisions that may result into allegations of favouritism. Thus, accepting the L1 bid (lowest bid) is the norm. Since L1 bidders may compromise on the quality and technical specifications, an attempt is made to assess a bid which is L1T1 (lowest in price and highest in technical quality). The "technical quality" is a subjective parameter and hence the decision of decision upon the "T1" is mostly left to the technical experts, e.g., the air force technicians, who could be the end users.

Price to win (discussed above) is a popular strategy for winning the government deals.

The governments have moved to e-tendering and e-procurement for most procurement of standardised items, to bring in more transparency and avoid getting embroiled in corruption controversies. The Government of India has, for example, set up a Central Public Procurement Portal for managing the tendering process, and a Government e-Marketplace (GeM) for procurement and selling of everyday use goods and services. Government of India has also set up e-auction portals so that the sellers can participate in the government procurement transparently.

Working with the government has its pluses and minuses. Dealing with various stakeholders in the government requires knowledge of the way they work. Hence some private businesses avoid bidding for government contracts or tenders. However, with proper guidance in bidding as well as subsequent delivery and collection process, this is a sector that could be profitable and generate substantial revenues. Government business is also relatively recession-proof since the governments may increase the spending during the recession, to stimulate demand and kick-off recovery cycle.

***Government pricing – Checklist:***

| | |
|---|---|
| 1 | Are you aware of the intricacies and complexities of working with the government, right from sales to delivery and collection of security deposit? |
| 2 | Have you identified the government departments and stakeholders that you would like to work with, and built a value proposition and pricing strategy for them? |
| 3 | Are you able to take advantages of economies of scale that most government contracts provide? |
| 4 | Are you ready to price the deal to win, while being acceptable on technical and commercial considerations? |
| 5 | Have you worked out the mode of participating in the government contracts, for example, tenders, e-tenders, e-procurement, e-auction etc.? |

## 7. Special Offers

Special offers are a popular way of advancing the buying decision of the customer by providing an incentive to act immediately. Diwali sales in India and Boxer's day sales in the USA are examples of special offers rolled out every year. Since the customers have now come to expect these sales, they at times postpone the decision to buy, so that they can buy at huge discounts on these special offers!

The top e-commerce players in India, Amazon and Flipkart, now offer special days on which a large number of products are offered at huge discounts. Some of the products that experience cyclical or seasonal declines in sales offer clearance sales during the off-season. The retailers routinely lower the prices of the items that are near the use-before (or use-by) date to incentivise customers into buying those before they have to be pulled off the shelf due to regulatory constraints.

Various stakeholders gather at industry exhibitions and trade fairs, and it is an opportunity for companies to offer discounts and develop new business relationships. Online stores offer special discounts for customers diverted from partner websites. Take-it-or-leave-it, on-the-spot offers also advance the buying decisions due to special discounted prices.

Special offers pricing is not restricted to the penetration pricing or introductory pricing. Special offer prices are made available in various ways throughout the lifecycle of the product:

1. Offers for a specific customer segment, e.g., members only
2. Offers for a specific period, e.g., the first week of February
3. Offers for a specific festival, e.g., Diwali season
4. Offers at a specific event, e.g., industry exhibition
5. Offers for sales through a particular channel partner, e.g., eCommerce portal
6. Offers for a specific product version, e.g., Kindle unlimited e-book
7. Offers for a particular mode of payment, e.g., payment via a specific bank's credit card
8. Offers in a specific retail outlet, e.g., outlets in a specific city
9. Offers to specific customer referrals, e.g., redirected from a partner website
10. Offers through a particular channel, e.g., own website

Special offers are very popular because they can be designed very creatively, and it is easier to revert back to the original pricing since the special offer announcements specifically convey the intent to the customers. The special offers are designed to mainly attract the new customers; however, unless it is possible to segregate them, old customers will also avail them and thus cannibalise the sales.

While special offers are a popular pricing strategy, the offers must be designed after careful analysis of the costs and benefits of running these offers. The benefits on account of the advancement of purchasing decision by the customers, new customer acquisition, increased member loyalty, development of partner network, lower investment in inventories, improved channel effectiveness, and early cash flow must be quantified. The costs are relatively easy to measure, as far as they relate to reduced prices or cost of freebies etc. However, the costs of cannibalisation of regular sales are difficult to estimate.

***Special offers pricing – Checklist:***

| | |
|---|---|
| 1 | Have you analysed the potential benefits of making special offers? |
| 2 | Have you analysed various modes of making those offers and decided on the optimum offers? |
| 3 | Have you analysed the costs of making special offers? |
| 4 | Have you estimated negative impact such as setting expectation of lower price in the mind of the customers and cannibalisation of sales at regular price? |

## 8. Guerrilla pricing

Guerrilla Marketing is defined as an advertising strategy that focuses on low-cost unconventional marketing tactics that yield maximum results. In practice, some of the close competitors have used the guerrilla tactics to compete head-on with each other through high pitched advertisement, feature-by-feature comparison of the products, and triggered a response that resembles a war.

One of the key components of guerrilla marketing is pricing. A brand which positions itself as a premium brand will never use guerrilla marketing tactics. The ones who use this will primarily emphasise on the lower price or a high value delivered with similar price.

In India, two major 2-wheeler manufacturers engaged in guerrilla marketing for months. Likewise, two detergent manufacturers used these tactics for some time. Two of the world's biggest cola brands involved in marketing and advertising campaigns that targeted each other, and simultaneously offered their products at low prices. Two of the biggest cab aggregators have used these tactics recently, mainly through pricing, in most cities across the world, including in India. Likewise, the food aggregators offered substantial discounts besides aggressive tie-ups with the restaurants and the zero-delivery charges offers. In all these cases, pricing was the key to the campaigns.

Guerrilla pricing is a part of overall guerrilla marketing strategy, which involves a promotional campaign using unconventional approach, such as high-pitched advertising, head-on targeting of the closest competitor, targeting the current customers of the nearest competitor through special offers and absorbing losses to onboard competitor's customers.

It is challenging to sustain guerrilla marketing and pricing for a long-term since both companies lose the money in the quest for market dominance. Except for the market leaders with deep pockets, this strategy doesn't make sense for the others.

***Guerrilla pricing – Checklist:***

| | |
|---|---|
| 1 | Have you identified the closest competitors whose customer base you want to target using the guerrilla marketing campaign? |
| 2 | Are you confident that pricing is key to achieving the goals of the guerrilla marketing campaign? |
| 3 | Are you able to anticipate the reaction of the competitors and have devised ways to overcome those counter-tactics? |
| 4 | Have you estimated the costs of running a guerrilla campaign and of special pricing to support that strategy? |
| 5 | Have you allocated budget to sustain the guerrilla campaign and pricing till the expected results are achieved, and backed up the budget with sufficient funds? |
| 6 | Have you analysed the impact of the campaign and the pricing tactics on the customer perception of the brand and the product? |

*"Nobody ever wins a price war – it's all about who survives the longest."*

***—Aki Kalliatakis***

## Comparison of Sales-driven Strategies

The table below compares various sales-driven strategies.

| *Criteria* | *Introductory* | *Benchmarking* | *Price to Win* | *Volume pricing* | *Auction pricing* | *Govt pricing* | *Special Offers* | *Guerrilla pricing* |
|---|---|---|---|---|---|---|---|---|
| Risk for vendor | Medium | Low | High | Low | Medium | Medium | Low | High |
| Risk for customer | Low | Low | Medium | Low | High | Low | Medium | Low |
| Usage in Projects pricing | Low | Medium | Medium | Low | Low | Medium | Low | Low |
| Usage in Products pricing | High | Medium | Low | High | High | Medium | High | High |
| Usage in Services pricing | High | High | High | Medium | Low | Low | Medium | Low |

| ***Criteria*** | ***Introductory*** | ***Benchmarking*** | ***Price to Win*** | ***Volume pricing*** | ***Auction pricing*** | ***Govt pricing*** | ***Special Offers*** | ***Guerrilla pricing*** |
|---|---|---|---|---|---|---|---|---|
| Usage in the B2B market | Medium | High | High | High | Medium | High | Medium | Low |
| Usage in the B2C market | High | Medium | Low | High | Medium | Low | High | Low |

*"There is scarcely anything in the world that some man cannot make a little worse, and sell a little more cheaply. The person who buys on price alone is this man's lawful prey."*

***—John Ruskin***

# CHAPTER *Ten*

## *Modern Strategies of Pricing*

*"The value of money comes from the private sector in the form of price for product, services rendered, what people are willing to pay for something they want or need. That's where value happens."*

***—Rush Limbaugh***

We classified pricing strategies into 5 broad categories – traditional, sales-driven, modern, risk-reward based and innovative. The "modern" strategies have evolved mostly in last two to three decades, driven by the internationalisation of markets, growth in the services sector, and increasing need for differentiation. Let's look at the advantages and limitations of following modern pricing strategies.

## Advantages of modern pricing strategies

1. Recognises pricing as a key to marketing
2. Caters to unique needs of services marketing
3. Opens up multiple channels for driving growth
4. Links pricing and revenues with costs
5. Focuses on delivering value to the customer

## Limitations of modern pricing strategies

1. Requires deeper understanding of customer

2. Must have a communication strategy in place
3. Widely used, hence not perceived as 'unique.'
4. Limited application to hi-tech, internet and e-commerce
5. Limited rewards from limited risk-taking

## Modern pricing strategies

Some of the critical modern pricing strategies include

1. Segment pricing
2. Referral Discounts
3. Add -ons
4. Marginal pricing
5. Geographical
6. White label pricing
7. Bundle pricing
8. Value driven

Let's look at the contemporary pricing strategies one by one.

## 1. Segment pricing

One-size-fits-all product and price are both things of the past. The product design teams now invariably come up with options to target broad customer segments to expand target market, increase revenues and increase profitability.

The marketing teams are therefore challenged with dividing target customers into segments that align with the product variant, set appropriate price and design launch offers. The segment, which is a prime focus and driver of sales and profitability, must find the desired product variant as the 'best value' option.

It is a matter of debate and individual choice, as to how many variants you should offer a customer within a segment? There is a consensus in the marketing community that not offering an opportunity amounts to a yes-or-no binary and hence must be avoided. Likewise, offering over 5 choices will confuse the customer, and the decision is likely to be postponed. Offering three options is generally consider adequate. Within the three choices offered, the one which the seller would prefer to be the best-seller is always designed to provide the best value while bringing in maximum profitability.

One of the additional ways of segmenting the customers is through offering a member-only price and product benefits. Ecommerce players and food aggregators offer member-only deals that give additional benefits, such as quicker delivery, free delivery, no-questions-asked returns, and so on. This incentivises the customers to become 'members' by paying a subscription which is typically monthly or annual. The membership fees is an additional source of revenue for these eCommerce companies. This strategy is also used by retailers with physical presence, hotels, airlines, travel aggregators and restaurants.

One more way of segmenting the customers is by co-branding and leveraging the reach of other players. The retailers, restaurants, hotels, airlines, travel aggregators, and eCommerce players issue co-branded credit cards or provide special discounts to the customers who pay through a specific payment option. The rewards programs of credit card issuers include redemptions in the form of free purchase from particular brands or discount coupons. The fact that the customer is eligible for these credit cards or uses the specific payment options helps segment those customers as likely high value and volume purchasers.

The online education, training and certification providers offer separate pricing for individuals, students and institutional subscribers. The purchasing power of the students, for example, is lower than the corporates and individuals. The corporates are likely to buy a higher number of individual subscriptions under the corporate subscription. The individuals are likely to purchase premium courses if they believe value is higher. Special offers to individuals are designed where multiple courses bought at the same time attract steep discount.

The segment-specific pricing can be implemented by categorising customers using criteria such as

1. Location – metros, cities, towns and villages; urban and rural; local and international
2. Age – school students, college-going students, postgraduate students

3. Education – illiterate, matriculates, graduates, postgraduates, higher education
4. Occupation – students, homemakers, workers, professionals, businessmen
5. Technology usage – early adopters, tech-savvy, tech-challenged
6. Hobbies – music, health & fitness enthusiasts, art lovers, writers

Each of these categories could be potential segments of customers for a specific product. Their buying habits, purchasing power, evaluation criteria and such other relevant aspects are crucial to pricing and branding.

***Segment pricing - Checklist***

| | |
|---|---|
| 1 | Have you categorised potential customers using identifiable and distinct criteria? |
| 2 | Do these customer segments have unique characteristics that can be leveraged to design better product variants, marketing campaigns and pricing strategies? |
| 3 | Do you have product variants that match the expectations and needs of these segments? |
| 4 | Does the segmentation help in enlarging the size of the addressable target market and improve profitability? |
| 5 | Does the cost of customer acquisition remain within the acceptable bounds because of the total lifetime value of the customer in a specific segment? |
| 6 | Do you have a system in place to regularly review the segmentation and revise those to ensure they remain in sync with the changing demographics? |

## 2. Referral Discounts

A satisfied customer is the best walking advertisement for a business. The businesses of the past grew mainly using word-of-mouth publicity. This worked well where the market was defined by physical boundaries, with select companies operating across multiple borders. How does one exploit customer loyalty to one's advantages in the diverse and extensive physical market, and the virtual world?

Offering discounts or reward points to the existing customers for their recommendation of the business or product resolves this challenge. The word-of-mouth is converted into a tangible coupon or a virtual one. The customer can easily gift this coupon to a friend, family or an associate. Once the purchase is made against the coupon, it can be traced back to the customer who gifted it, and that customer can be rewarded. Nowadays, customers can generate referrals virtually using a website or a mobile phone app and share with their family and friends.

The chances of a friend or a family member signing-up or buying are much higher because of close relationship with the person referring to the business or a product. That is, this source has the best conversion ratio of a prospect to a customer. Additionally, the cost of customer acquisition using referrals as a channel is, in most cases, the lowest.

Low cost, coupled with high conversion chances makes this a favourite sales strategy. Hence businesses that focus on referrals generation have come up, including mobile apps driven referral networks, that allow companies to generate referral coupons, and give rewards based on the sale. Mobile App driven businesses, e.g., food aggregators, routinely provide rewards to the members (customers) for referrals.

The discount coupons and referral rewards are more appropriate for B2C market; a variant of this strategy, "finder's fees", is used in B2B businesses as compared to B2B marketers, to encourage business to refer clients.

***Referral discounts - Checklist***

| | |
|---|---|
| 1 | Is there a scope for using discount coupons/ referral rewards in your business? |
| 2 | Are any of your competitors using these? If yes, how is it working out for them? |
| 3 | Have you analysed your conversion ratios and cost of customer acquisition through other modes and compared with the discount coupons/ referral rewards program? |
| 4 | Do you have a system in place to track coupons/ referrals and measure the performance as well as costs? |
| 5 | Are you able to track how much of your revenue is being cannibalised because of your customers using discount coupons or generating cross-referrals? |

## 3. Add –ons

"Add-ons" are typically the special offers made to the customers who merely needs a 'nudge' to justify the buying decision to himself or other stakeholders. These are usually predetermined products and services which the salesperson, at the end of the negotiation, reserves in his armour.

Every customer may not expect a giveaway. Some decide to buy after careful evaluation and need no further incentive. However, some customers genuinely face a dilemma or are doubting their decision-making skill. A last-minute add-on or a giveaway makes a vast difference in their decision.

The new-age technology giants and fully online services providers have also mimicked the salesperson's tactics. The world's biggest professionals networking site offers you a special discount for a few months when you try to cancel the subscription at the end of the one-month trial period. The idea to get the customer used to the subscriber-only features for more time and increased the probability of his continuing after using the site for a few more months. The trial offer is itself offered again after a few months or a year.

One of the leading sites offering tools for creating graphic designs also uses a similar strategy. A special discounted price is provided for long-term if one attempts to cancel the subscription at the end of the trial period. Since the subscriber is already 'primed' with a higher price for a regular subscription, the chances of accepting the special discounted offer are very high.

***Add-ons - Checklist***

| | |
|---|---|
| 1 | Have you identified the customer buying points and concerns that may hold back the buying decision? |
| 2 | Have you worked out the add-ons or giveaways that would favourably impact the customer's decision without impacting profitability? |
| 3 | In case you deliver your product or service online, have you configured your add-ons or giveaways to achieve maximum conversion and revenues? |

## 4. Marginal pricing

The marginal cost of production is the cost of producing an additional unit of a product. The product, if sold at a net price below the marginal cost, results in a gross loss to the business. It doesn't make sense selling a product below the marginal cost. The better alternative is not to produce the product and thus avoid the loss.

Costs of producing and delivering a product are mainly classified as fixed costs and variable costs. The fixed costs remain the same regardless of the level of production. E.g., if a manufacturing plant for producing tube-lights is setup at Rs 20 crores, the fixed costs of Rs 20 crores are "sunk' once and for all, regardless of how many tube-lights are produced. Some of the items like lease rent for the factory land should also be counted as "fixed costs", though they are paid month on month, since they remain the same, regardless of how many tube-lights are produced. Some of the costs are in the nature of fixed-variable costs, i.e., they are fixed up to a certain level of production but change once that level is breached. The relationship between these costs, revenue and profitability, are depicted below.

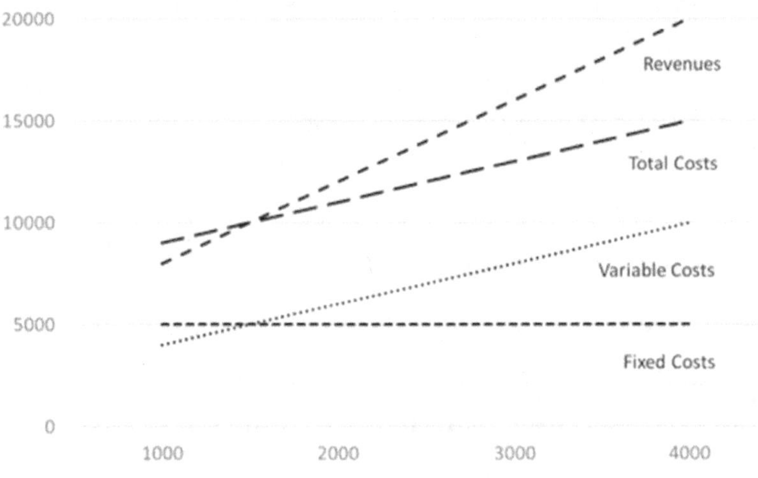


The volume of production and sale at which the fixed costs are fully recovered is the point at which the business starts making real profit if the price is maintained above the marginal costs. This point is called "break-even point" in accounting jargon. Once this volume is reached, the business benefits by selling additional production at a price higher than, but close to the marginal cost. This strategy of pricing products close to the marginal cost is called "marginal pricing" strategy. Manufacturers in countries like China have frequently been accused of "dumping" products in markets like USA, by selling at artificially low prices aboard, while selling at a high price domestically, thus recovering full fixed costs.

Marginal pricing is one of the predatory pricing strategies like guerrilla pricing and cannot be sustained in the long run. The cost leadership position what enables marginal pricing cannot be maintained as a strategic advantage over the long term.

***Marginal pricing - Checklist***

| | |
|---|---|
| 1 | Do you have a robust accounting system in place for identifying fixed, semi-variable and variable costs of production? |
| 2 | Are you able to segregate customers for offering two different prices without cannibalising the profitable segment? |
| 3 | Have you assessed the likely price war that marginal pricing is expected to set in the target market, with competition taking up guerrilla pricing strategy? |

## 5. Geographical

One of the ways of segmenting the customers is by geography in which the customer makes the purchase. The geographical segmentation could be made within a city, a state, a country or beyond. Within India, the products in cities like Pune, Bengaluru and Mumbai are priced higher compared to other cities in India. Across the international borders, most products are priced after evaluating the purchasing power of the target customer segment in the local currency.

The international prices are often quoted by the seller free-on-board (FOB), i.e., the price at which the products will be supplied to the point of loading in a carrier for cross-border transport. The quote is in the local currency of the seller, or in the US dollars, which dominates international trade.

Besides purchasing power, the following impact the geographical pricing decisions

1. Local manufacturing costs – which impact the competitors' prices to an extent
2. Transportation costs – of shipping to another geography
3. Currency conversion rates – when sold across the international borders
4. Local taxes – that impact the landed cost of items that the customer pays
5. Import duties – that impact the landed costs of the imported products
6. Export incentives – that help exporters price the product competitively
7. Payment and settlement mechanisms – that impact the cost of transaction and risks
8. Product complexity – which affects the add-on services that the customer may need

One of the reasons the multinational companies set up manufacturing bases, in the markets that are important to them, is to ensure that the cost of manufacturing is in line with the local purchasing price and costs and prices of the locally manufactured products. In most cases, government subsidies are available for local jobs creation, which help lower the cost of production.

The fully digital products are produced once and consumed multiple times. The delivery cost is low. Hence the flexibility in pricing is very high. Massive Open Online Courses (MOOCs) are usually sold at a lesser price for customers in countries like India, where purchasing power is relatively lower, compared to countries like the USA. There is no difference in the product delivered. One of the reasons for the popularity of digital delivery mode like Kindle delivery for the books is that the costs of production and delivery are almost zero. Likewise, the total cost of subscribing to business applications that are delivered over the internet and hosted on a cloud, are substantially lower, because the geographical location of the user is immaterial.

Within domestic markets, some of the products are sold at uniform prices regardless of the delivery location. This is made possible because of the emergence of courier companies that cover several destinations. However, this may also mean that there is a cross-subsidisation in favour of buyers in remote locations.

***Geographical pricing - Checklist***

| | |
|---|---|
| 1 | Have you analysed the scope for geographical pricing for your products and services by evaluating the production and delivery costs, transportation costs, taxes and duties, and such other relevant costs? |
| 2 | Have you considered the impact of the purchasing power of the local currency of the customer on the product buying decision? |
| 3 | Have you explored the option of reducing the costs of delivery to remote geographies by options like producing locally, developing logistics infrastructure or delivering electronically? |
| 4 | Do you have a clear idea of how geographical pricing impacts your profitability and cash flows? |

## 6. White label pricing

The ability of a well-managed brand to pull in sales and profitability is well known. The branded products command higher sales and better price since the customers can count on the brand owner to invest in maintaining and enhancing the brand through quality products and services.

The big retail brands which grew in the last three to four decades achieved their growth riding on the back of branded products. Once the retailers expanded considerably, their regular customers started valuing the retailer's brand as much as the other brands being sold at the retail outlets. The retailers controlled the last step in the supply chain and came up with the of the idea of selling products under their brand. Thus, the concept of white- labelling came up in significant way.

White labelling involves a reputed brand supplying the products to the retailers or others without identifying the brand on the product. The buyer, in turn, adds his brand and sells the product under that brand. Since the product is usually purchased in large quantities, the retailers get volume discounts. With the retail customers slowly warming up to the idea of a retailer's brand, they are willing to buy these products.

White labelling works because the manufacturers enjoy the economies of scale from large production volume and therefore can sell to the retailers or others at a relatively lower price. They don't have to incur massive investment in the supply chain or marketing ad sales. The retailer, having already invested in the procurement chain and retail outlets, ensure zero to low additional investment in procuring, stocking and selling the white-labelled products under their brand. The end consumers are also happy because they get quality products at relatively lower prices.

Over the long term, the branded products face a severe threat from large retailers selling white-labelled products, since the retailers have an "unfair" advantage of bulk volumes and direct reach. White labelling, as a concept, also works in projects driven industries where the main contractor, a large and reputed firm, bids for a contract, and in turn ties up with smaller contractors for executing parts of the contract.

White label pricing is also being used for intangible pricing products like business applications. E.g., travel agents use a white-labelled platform for creating products (travel plans), rolling out offers, managing their websites, and providing self-service capabilities to customers like directly booking hotels and air tickets.

White-label product manufacturer focuses on product design and manufacturing while saving on the costs of marketing the product. White label pricing has opened up opportunities for making one's product available to the competitors and benefiting from the economies of scale. The white labelled product, however, cannibalises the sales of the manufacturer, if they market the product under their brand. Hence this trade-off has to be carefully evaluated.

***White label pricing - Checklist***

| | |
|---|---|
| 1 | Have you analysed the scope for selling the product under your own brand, as an alternative to selling it as a white-labelled product? |
| 2 | Have you calculated the long-term benefit of building its own brand than sell the white-labelled product in the market? |
| 3 | Does white-label pricing for sales to competitors ensure benefit from economies of scale besides profitability on sale or recovery of fixed costs through marginal pricing? |

| | |
|---|---|
| 4 | Have you analysed the impact on the sale of own branded product because of cannibalisation from the sale of competing product by the competitor? |
| 5 | Are you able to sell the product under your own brand simultaneously with adequate differentiation that drives superior profits? |

## 7. Bundle Pricing

The bundle pricing is a strategy used to make the product more attractive and useful for the customer, sell additional product along with the other, make the bundled products unique and challenging to compare with others and reduce the cost of customer acquisition. The bundled pricing can also be used to introduce new products to the customer along with the products he is used to buying.

The bundle pricing is used across industries, from legacy to the modern. Razors and after-shave lotions are bundled with shaving creams. The restaurants offer buffet menus along with an option of a-la-carte. Fast-food chains like McDonald and KFC provide meals that include multiple items on the menu. Retailers sell mobile phones with data plans and accessories like screen protectors and covers. Projectors and projection screens are sold together. Laptops are sold with carrying bags or a sleeve. Laptops and computers are sold with and without operating system as two options. After the slowdown in real estate sales (post the 2008 global financial crisis), many real estate developers offer freebies like cars, TVs and other electronic items, along with the homes, which makes the bundle attractive to the buyers.

With the convergence of communication towards mobile phones, the telecom operators are offering plans that combine phone data, voice/ VOIP calls, broadband internet, and subscription to TV and entertainment content providers. The bundled pricing is popular in online selling through websites and eCommerce websites. When you add an item to your shopping cart, the eCommerce sites suggest "frequently bought together" product bundles. These bundles are automatically created based on shopping history of a large number of buyers, and therefore, the likelihood of the customer opting for the bundle are higher.

The bundles are always priced attractively, such that prices of individual items in the package if bought separately are higher. Creative bundling of products, which otherwise have to compete for products readily available, make the deal unique and challenging to compare with the competitors.

The bundled pricing is being as such being leveraged to

1. Create a 'unique' product offering
2. Solve the same problem or need of the customer
3. Make price comparison difficult
4. Leverage leader-pricing (loss-leader pricing) for popular products

5. Cross-sell and up-sell other products and
6. Reduce the cost of customer acquisition

However, the bundled pricing strategy is easy to replicate and may lose differentiation quickly. Also, when a customer buys a product in a bundle at a lower cost, the sale of the same product on a stand-alone basis at a higher price is cannibalised. One prominent example of the cannibalisation of a product is a toothbrush. With almost every toothpaste brand selling a toothpaste bundled with a "free" toothbrush, the sales of separate toothbrush have been cannibalised to a great extent.

***Bundle pricing - Checklist***

| | |
|---|---|
| 1 | Do you have a portfolio of products that can be logically bundled together to solve the same problem or need of the customer? |
| 2 | Have you analysed which are the products that have high potential for cross-selling by bundling together? |
| 3 | Have you investigated whether the bundled pricing can be lowered in comparison to the separate sale of both the products, to make it attractive to the customers? |
| 4 | Have you analysed the impact of product-bundle pricing on sales, profitability and brand perception, by considering lower pricing, advanced purchase, reduced cost of delivery, and reduced cost of customer acquisition? |
| 5 | Have you analysed the potential adverse impact from cannibalisation of the sales of the product in a bundle, and reduced profitability from cannibalisation? |

## 8. Value-based

Value-based pricing exercise focuses on aligning the price with the value delivered. The value, in the eyes of the customer, is subjective. Hence this alignment is challenging.

The same product or service, when delivered to a different customer segment, may be perceived to be of a higher or lower value. Let's take the example of a workshop conducted by a Human Resources consultant for developing awareness of the need for succession planning and coming up with a strategy for developing next generation of leadership. The same workshop, delivered by the same consultant, using an in a similar approach, maybe valued highly by a large family-owned and managed company that wants to professionalise and grow more significant, as compared to the value assigned by a small business owner, who intends to pass on the ownership to his children.

The value of a product for the customer could also change with time, location and consumption pattern. The umbrellas and raincoats have a higher value at the onset of the monsoon, and sweaters and mufflers, at the onset of the winter. Dark glasses are more valuable in the summer. A cold drink is more valuable to the same customer at a holiday destination in summer, as compared to his residence. Tourists pay a high price for a professional photograph printed on-demand at a tourist location. An alcoholic beverage is more valuable in a pub, with great ambience and the company of friends. A branded product with premium positioning, say a branded watch, is perceived to be of higher value, simply because it conveys the higher 'status' of the user.

The fundamental reason the product design teams are tasked with the responsibility of coming up with multiple variants or versions of a product is to differentiate value delivered and charge a commensurate price to the customer. These variants help capture broader customer segment and also enhance profitability. Value-based pricing, therefore, allows you to develop product that add higher value to the customer, and even profit from the same, by positioning to the appropriate customer segment.

One of the long-established tea brands in India has recently opened tea outlets on the lines of the coffee chains that have popularised the concept worldwide. In those outlets, they sell tea at 10x the price of the tea sold by the roadside tea shop. They justify the 10x price through overall "experience" of having the tea at their outlet, as compared to a usual restaurant. Thus, the price point has been elevated substantially by delivering better experience that the customer values highly.

*"The product's value is the sum total of all functional and hedonic benefits derived by the customer from the product's bundle of features."*

***—Utpal Dholakia***

Value-based pricing has almost become indispensable in the business- to -business markets since the decision-makers in the customer organisation are usually required to justify the buying decision using numbers. Articulating value delivered and using it as a key differentiator vis-a-vis the competitors should be a part of every sales playbook.

Value-based pricing is, however, complicated in products that the customers are used to treating as a 'commodity'. E.g., the staple food of the local communities usually sells at a lower price, in comparison to 'exotic' food from remote locations. There is relatively less scope for differentiating products that are considered daily necessities, as compared to the items that are one-off purchased luxury items. E.g., grocery items versus a TV set.

***Value-based pricing - Checklist***

| | |
|---|---|
| 1 | Does your product design goal explicitly involve creating different product variants that deliver distinct value to different customer segments? |
| 2 | Are you able to articulate and differentiate value delivered to the specific customer segment by a specific product variant? |
| 3 | Have you considered nurturing different brands for positioning and pricing the product variants that offer highly differentiated value proposition? |
| 4 | Do you have in place, a mechanism for evaluating the value derived by the customer from different product variants, and accordingly price the options? |

| 5 | Does the value-based design and pricing strategy help you target a bigger customer base and drive higher profits on a portfolio level? |
|---|---|

## Comparison of modern Strategies

The table below compares various modern strategies.

| *Criteria* | *Segment Pricing* | *Referral Discounts* | *Add-ons* | *Marginal pricing* | *Geographic* | *White Label pricing* | *Bundle Pricing* | *Value-driven* |
|---|---|---|---|---|---|---|---|---|
| Risk for vendor | Low | Medium | Medium | Medium | Low | Medium | Low | Low |
| Risk for customer | Low | Low | Low | Low | Low | Low | Low | Low |
| Usage in Projects pricing | Medium | Low | Low | Low | Medium | Medium | Medium | Medium |
| Usage in Products pricing | High | High | High | High | High | High | High | High |
| Usage in Services pricing | High | Medium | Medium | Low | High | Low | Medium | Medium |
| Usage in the B2B market | Medium | Low | Low | High | High | Low | Medium | High |
| Usage in the B2C market | High | High | High | Medium | High | High | High | Low |

*"People want economy and they will pay any price to get it."*

***—Lee Iacocca***

# CHAPTER *Eleven*

## *Risk-Reward Based Pricing Strategies*

*"Perhaps the reason price is all your customers care about is because you haven't given them anything else to care about."*

***—Seth Godin***

We classified pricing strategies into five broad categories – traditional, sales-driven, modern, risk-reward based and innovative. The "risk-reward" based strategies have evolved in the business- to- business markets, inspired by the need to differentiate with the competitors, by assuring the customers that you have a stake in the success of their business. Let's look at the advantages and limitations of following risk-reward based pricing strategies.

## Advantages of risk-reward based pricing strategies

1. Encourages creativity and innovation in product design
2. Forces identification of customers with high lifetime value
3. Establishes linkages between price and value
4. Helps move from a vendor to "business-partner" status
5. Focuses on growth by quantifying results

## Limitations of risk-reward based pricing strategies

1. Risk-taking appetite is a prerequisite
2. Requires in-depth analysis of customer's business
3. Requires deeper understanding of trends in customer's industry
4. Exposes business to the risks of customer's performance
5. Requires expertise in financial modelling and data analysis

## Risk-reward based pricing strategies

Some of the critical risk-reward based pricing strategies include

1. One-time license
2. License & Renewal
3. Free trial
4. ROI based
5. Pricing product co-creation
6. Pricing for product validation
7. Money-Back Guarantees
8. Transaction based
9. Goals - linked

Let's look at the risk-reward based pricing strategies one by one.

## 1. One-time license

Granting a one-time license for using a product for a lifetime makes it easier for the customer to calculate costs and benefits. Since the costs are one-time, and if the bonus can be calculated for a foreseeable time in future with reasonable accuracy, the decision-making is easy. The vendor, on the other hand, clearly knows the revenue and has to forecast future costs with reasonable certainty.

Many off-the-shelf software product vendors worked on the one-time licensing strategy about a decade back. Microsoft, for example, used to sell the licenses for the Windows Operating System and the Office suite of products by charging one-time fees. These products needed continuous changes in the form of bug-fixes, compatibility and feature additions.

Since the licensing was one-time, the cost of delivering changes could not be passed on to the customers; they had to be estimated and factored into the original one-time licensing fees. Once the changes accumulated to a major change from the original version, a new product version release was planned, and the earlier release was made obsolete by withdrawing support over a period of time.

There are examples of brands that grant one-time franchise license to the partners for the use of brand name, credentials, process and technology, with no payments involved after that, except for arms-length procurement of products or services from the brand licensor. The franchise owner is thus assured of lifetime use with no further obligation. However, there is not an incentive for the brand owner to nurture the brand in future by making more investments, hence the brand may lose the appeal, impacting the franchise owner adversely.

The product yields revenue one-time over its life and costs are incurred over the lifetime. Thus, the vendor (licensor) carries the risk of cost running higher than forecasted. In contrast, the customer (licensee) carries the risk of the product being made obsolete earlier than expected. Vendor, however, benefits from a massive inflow of cash upfront more shortly in the product's usage period, and the risk from customer attrition is zero. This is being achieved by charging a very high one-time lifetime licensing price with no guarantee how long the product will be supported.

***One-time license - Checklist***

| | |
|---|---|
| 1 | Does your product or a key component derive value from intellectual property that is allowed for use against price? |
| 2 | Can the product or component be approved for unlimited period use against one-time licensing cost? |
| 3 | Have you worked out the costs of supporting the product during its active use? |
| 4 | Do you have a plan to nudge the customers into buying the next version of the product at additional cost, when it comes up? |

## 2. License & Renewal

The one-time licensing strategy is losing its popularity. It is being replaced with the upfront licensing plus annual license renewal and yearly maintenance contracts.

The annual license renewal is typically a percentage of the upfront license price, say 20%. Tus, if there are product variants with different upfront license price, the annual renewal is also in line with the same, since it is stated in percentage. The yearly renewal is expected to cover the cost of hosting, bug-fixes, performance improvements and essential feature additions.

The annual maintenance is involved where the users need support. This is more relevant for the business software, where uptime, as well as functionality, has an impact on the business operations. The annual maintenance is usually offered in variants with the response and resolution times are linked to the variant. E.g., a platinum plan has the fastest response and resolution time assurance as compare to the gold plan and the silver plan.

The franchise licenses are typically granted to the partners for the use of brand name, credentials, process and technology, by asking for the upfront large franchise fee and a portion of revenue thereafter. The large food chains like McDonalds, KFC, Pizza Hut and many others follow this model. The upfront licensing fees is a part of initial investment by the franchise owner. The following prices (royalty or license revenue) is typically a percentage of the revenue and a percentage of revenue contribution towards the advertisement budget for the local market. Additionally, the brand owner supplies the raw material to the franchise owner and makes profits on that. In some cases, the original license is valid for a few years and has to be renewed after a few years at substantial cost.

The fact that the brand owner continues to profit from licensing the brand makes it imperative for them to nurture the brand. Thus, the franchise owner is assured of the brand being relevant in future because of investments made by the brand owner.

The annual license renewal and the annual maintenance provide sustained revenues for the vendor to take care of the costs of product enhancements, bug-fixes, hosting, and other activities. Since these costs may rise over the period of time, it is better to have a clause in the contract that provides for a reset in the amount after a few years.

The upfront license price combined with the annual renewal and maintenance is an accessible mode of providing online tools and applications. The risk to the vendor is minimized through cash flows in the future. The customer retains the option of discontinuing the product, thus minimizing the risk involved in paying the full price through a one-time license.

***License plus Renewal - Checklist***

| | |
|---|---|
| 1 | Does your product or a key component derive value from intellectual property that is allowed for use against price? |
| 2 | Have you worked out the price break-up into the upfront license and periodic renewal, after considering the time value of money? |
| 3 | Have you worked out the costs of supporting the product during its active use? Does the periodic renewal cover these costs? |
| 4 | Do your customers need support beyond mere bug-fixes and performance improvements? If yes, have you worked out the maintenance price with variants that are linked to performance (such as response and resolution times)? |

## 3. Free trial

Under a free trial, the customer is entitled to return the product and demand return of price paid if he is not satisfied with the product. Hence extending the free trial offer to the customer requires a lot of confidence in the product. However, it is also a great way to get more and more customers to try the product and experience the benefits.

Free trial for a limited period reduces the customer's money-risk to zero and limits the time-risk since the customer can decide to return the product sooner and go for an alternative. The risk of offering a free trial is with the vendor. However, if the vendor has confidence in the product, the risk of returns after the free trial period is very low. If the item is usually purchased at a higher frequency, offering a free trial is a great option, since the free trial is needed only once, and the benefit of converting to a lifetime customer is much higher.

In some cases, the free trial option requires you to sign-up upfront for a subscription which gets kicked-in if you don't cancel the free trial after the trial period. This strategy ensures that it is easier for the customer to simply continue to be a paying customer at the end of the free trial, without having to take any action (such as swiping a credit card). However, the initial acquisition of the customer for a free trial may become difficult since the customers are reluctant to sign up without experiencing upfront.

The free trial option, however, may not be feasible in all cases. If the cost of delivering the product, accepting the Return, reprocessing and selling again is very high, free trials may be uneconomical. Also, if the item's integrity is compromised by allowing the usage (e.g., food, medicine or inner-ware product), a free trial cannot be offered.

A free trial is a very popular pricing strategy where the product delivery costs and negligible and the profitability is high once the customer makes a purchase. The online content providers like Netflix use the free trial strategy in a big way. It is also used by other content providers that provide online skill-building courses, where the courses are offered free for a limited period from subscription and charged later. At times, the courses are free, and the only certification is chargeable.

Free trial allows the customer to enjoy the full benefits of usage of the product for limited period; it differs from 'freemium', a recently evolved strategy, that allows for a lifetime benefit from utilization of limited functionality.

***Free Trial - Checklist***

| | |
|---|---|
| 1 | Is your product suitable for providing a free trial option without compromising on the integrity of the product? |
| 2 | Is the free trial a prerequisite for a customer to appreciate the product benefits? |
| 3 | Have you analysed the cost of providing free trial and compared with the benefits of increased conversion rates? |
| 4 | Do you have in place a mechanism to identify prospects who want to evaluate the product seriously and therefore likely to buy after the trial period if happy? |
| 5 | Have you compared free trial with alternative pricing strategies such as add-ons and freemium (explained elsewhere)? |

## 4. ROI based

Value-based pricing is one of the modern pricing strategies. The value delivered can be translated into numbers to arrive at the "return" the customer gets by investing in a product or a service. The Return and the investment numbers are used to calculate the Return on Investment

(ROI) which justifies the customer's buying decision. The customer can quantify ROI on various available options and buy the product that makes best business sense.

The vendor may additionally offer the customer a price which is linked to the Return earned by the customer. The higher the Return or business benefit, the higher price. If the customer is not able to get a higher business benefit as originally expected, he pays less. Thus, the vendor is sharing the risk that the customer faces. This not only lowers the cost and risk for the customer, this also establishes the credentials of the vendor as a "business partner" who has a "skin in the game". Also, if the customer derives higher business benefit, the vendor can generate higher profit. This higher profit is an incentive for the vendor to take the risk.

This strategy can be leveraged in pricing projects. The project delays can cause substantial loss to the customer such as delay in the start of completion of the other projects that are dependent, delay in starting production, and thus delay in revenue and cash flows. Most of the Engineering, Procurement and Construction (EPC) contracts, therefore, embed penalty clauses for the delay in execution caused by factors that are in the vendor's control. One of the powerful ways of ensuring that the contracts are completed in time or well ahead of time it to incorporate a clause that rewards the vendor for early completion.

In business-to-business markets, it is possible to quantify ROI in most deals. Even benefits of intangibles like training for the workforce or leaders can be quantified by using appropriate criteria, such as increased productivity on the job, reduced errors, reduced absenteeism, higher compliance with organizational norms, improved profitability on deals, higher retention (or lower attrition), improved punctuality, reduced defects, reduced customer complaints, increase in number of staff obtaining certification from independent bodies and so on.

The vendors should suggest the reward for early completion and base the calculation of reward on the business benefit derived by the customer from early go-to-market. A one- month early completion can be translated into additional revenue and profitability from one-month production, to which the reward can be linked. This strategy benefits both the parties and links risk with reward very well.

***ROI based pricing - Checklist***

| | |
|---|---|
| 1 | Does your target customer assess ROI before making a decision to buy your product or service? |
| 2 | Do you have a clear idea of the benefits that the customer expects to get by buying the product or service? |
| 3 | Are you able to quantify the benefits derived by the customers by using the product and the costs (investment) incurred for buying and using the product? |

| | |
|---|---|
| 4 | Do you have an appetite for pricing the product in line with the actual ROI obtained by the customer from using the product or service? |
| 5 | Will ROI linked price act as a differentiator that will increase your conversion ratio without comprising on the profitability? |

## 5. Pricing product co-creation

A product design approach that enables innovation should ideally involve the customer in the entire process. The customer involvement in the co-creation and build stage will help ensure that the product is functionality rich and user-friendly.

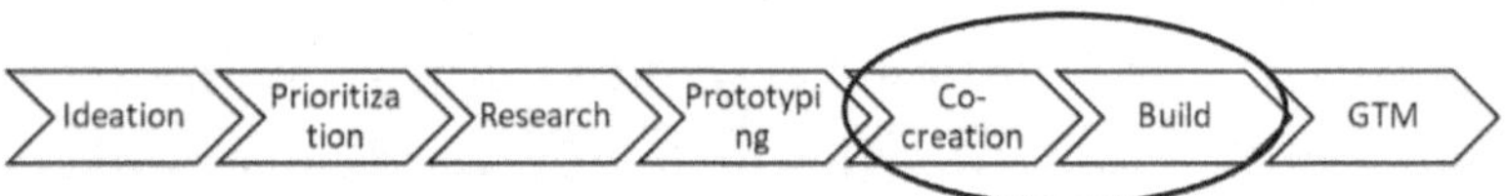


Most large and complex products are developed jointly with customers. The leading enterprise systems were designed with some of the customers who needed a particular functionality to manage their business. While developing a product jointly with the customer care must be taken to see that the product design is flexible enough to accommodate variations needed by the other customers. The intellectual property (IP) should be contractually retained by the vendor, else selling the product to other customers could invite litigation from the customer for whom the product was first developed.

The initial development where customer helps co-creation should be priced such that the customer gets the additional benefit of participating in the co-creation. The benefit of customer involvement would be monetized by selling the product off-the-shelf with minimum customization to the subsequent customers.

The product development cost, which is towards developing intellectual property (IP) for subsequent sale, should be capitalized. The special pricing worked out for the customer to incentivize them in participating in the product development process versus the usual price that would have been worked out for the deal also represents a notional investment in building the intellectual property.

***Pricing product co-creation - Checklist***

| | |
|---|---|
| 1 | Have you analysed the benefit of co-creating a product with a customer and monetizing the IP for creating a subsequent revenue pipeline? |
| 2 | Are you able to assess the incentive that will motivate the customer to participate in the product co-creation process? |
| 3 | Does the co-created product have a larger market? |
| 4 | Do you have in place a mechanism and skills to build the product such that it can be used by the other customers without major changes? |
| 5 | Have you ensured through a proper legally vetted contract that the IP for the co-created product belongs to you and can be sold on own without any objection by the customer who participated in the co-creation process? |

# 6. Pricing for product validation

Most entrepreneurs are successful initially in selling to the businesses run by people who know them. The previous relationship is an important factor that weighs in their favour in the sales process. However, getting a first customer beyond this initial circle of trust is a big challenge for most new businesses.

In order to develop sales traction, getting good customer referrals and case studies is imperative. This would mean getting those initial customers signed up and using the product sooner. Making a special offer to a set of customers to help get validation for the product is a good strategy in this case.

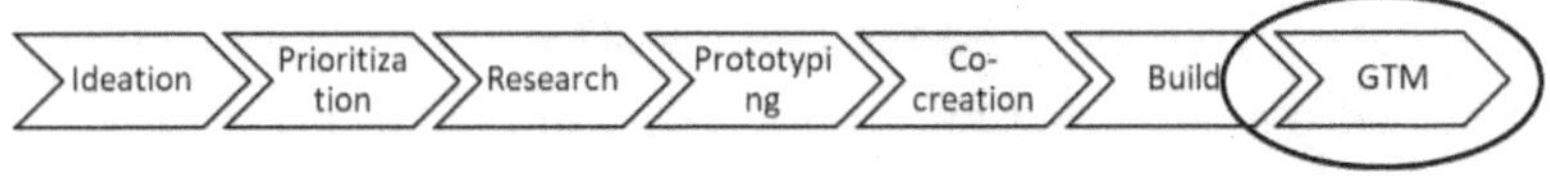


These initial set of customers may be offered a special price and provided with special add-ons. The lower revenue and additional costs are justified on the based on enhanced sales. If signing up a few initial customers by offering special prices is able to advance the go-to-market and customer acquisition by a few months, it is a benefit which should be factored in a while pricing for the first set of customers.

Offering special pricing to the initial few customers could provide the following advantages:

1. Validation of product functionality and usability
2. Establishing scalability and performance of the product
3. Enhancement of functionality considered critical
4. Credentials, word of mouth publicity, case studies and referrals
5. Quantification of business benefits delivered and ROI
6. Fine-tuning of the manufacturing, delivery and implementation process

***Pricing for product validation - Checklist***

| | |
|---|---|
| 1 | Have you assessed how you will sign up the initial customers, and what buying objections they may have? |
| 2 | Have you assessed whether offering the product at low/ negligible price, or free, will incentivize the customers to buy? |
| 3 | Have you assessed the total life cycle cost of production, delivery, implementation, support and maintenance of the products sold to the initial customers for product validation? |
| 4 | Do the faster go-to-market, higher conversions and accelerated revenues and cash flows justify making special pricing offers to the initial customers for product validation? |

## 7. Money-Back Guarantees

The no-questions-asked money-back guarantee also works as a free trial offer. However, the money-back guarantee is usually offered to resolve customer fears of the non-usability of fitness for use or defect in the product.

In case the customer is offered a money-back guarantee, the payment is collected upfront from the customer. When the customer makes the payment upfront, it is proof of his seriousness in trying out the product. Also, the emotional commitment to fulfil the transaction is higher. Chances of product return and claim for money-back are relatively lower in such cases, as compared to the free trial offers.

Money-back guarantees are offered for a very short period of time, whereas, product guarantees are provided for a longer but limited period of time, and these assure free repairs or replacement. Adding warranties that assure repairs for defects in the products helps assure the customers of the manufacturer's commitment to quality. Selling extended warranties beyond the initial manufacturer's warranties is a good source of additional revenue.

Money-back guarantees are provided by hotels, airlines, e-commerce players, retailers and many more businesses, and are rather popular today. The e-commerce players offer the no-questions-asked money-back on a large number of products based on the understanding of the customer. They find a huge increase in conversions since the delivery and pick up are managed by them at the customer doorstep.

However, the usefulness of money-back guarantees in attracting the customers should be carefully analysed.

The customers may not want the hassle of paying upfront, trying the product, claiming money back and then waiting for the money to be actually returned. Thus, the chances of conversion are lower.

***Money-back guarantees - Checklist***

| | |
|---|---|
| 1 | Have you assessed the need for providing assured money-back guarantees to the customers to increase the conversion rates? |
| 2 | Do you have a system in place to track and verify the product returns? |
| 3 | Do you have a system in place for processing money-back transactions? |

## 8. Transaction based

Transaction-based pricing, also at times called "pay-per-drink", is one of the most innovative risk-reward based pricing strategies that came up recently. The transaction-based pricing strategy allows the customer to link the payment for the product to the actual usage.

Take an example of a person using a payment gateway to see merchandise on his website. Most payment gateways do not charge upfront fees for embedding their applications in your website. The configuration is also made easy using appropriate design and interfaces. The user is charged the commission only for the transactions executed through the payment gateway, usually worked out as a percentage of the amount transacted and a flat fees per transaction.

On the vendor's part the cost of producing, maintaining and delivering the product is being charged to the customers over a period of usage rather than an upfront price. Additionally, the price charged itself is worked out based on the usage of the product, on which the vendor has no control. Thus, the vendor takes a much higher risk in pricing product using this strategy. As such, an expectation of higher reward is built in the transaction. The customer, on the other hand, needs low or negligible upfront investment, and also bears the low risk from overpricing, since it is linked to the usage. The higher the business volume, the higher the payment for the product, and vice versa.

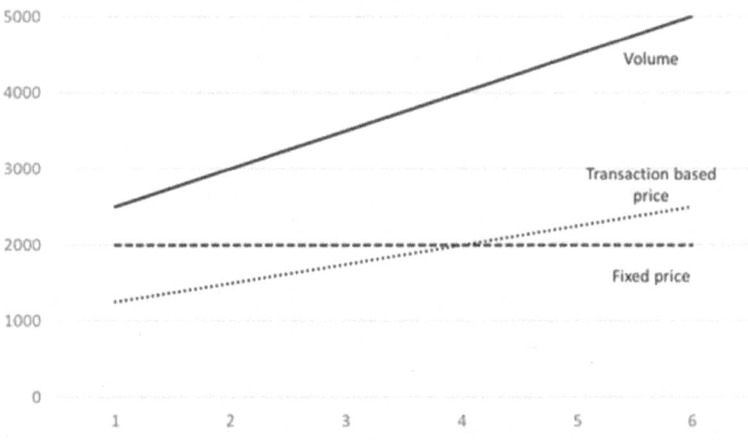


Some of the vehicle insurance companies are charging premium based on the miles driven. This means, an individual who uses his car less frequently will pay a lower premium, as compared to the static annual premium. In turn, the insurer's risk is reduced since most claims arise from damages caused while the vehicle is on the road.

The products that need low or negligible cost of delivery of additional unit are best suited for transaction-based pricing. Some of the leading platform providers in financial services charge transaction-based price to the banks and investment banks. The trend has caught up and is growing across industries.

***Transaction -based pricing - Checklist***

| | |
|---|---|
| 1 | Are you able to identify the right customers who would help you generate adequate revenue through the transaction-based pricing mechanism? |
| 2 | Are the target customers matured enough to understand the benefits and risks of signing up for the transaction-based pricing deal? |
| 3 | Does the product have enough stickiness that the customer will continue to use it when the transaction volume crosses the threshold where the cost of acquiring the product outright or another pricing model for a similar product makes more business sense? |
| 4 | Have you analysed the costs to the customer of switching over to another product and are those costs high enough for the customer to continue to use the product on the transaction-based pricing model? |
| 5 | Have you analysed the risks of pricing the product on the basis of transactions and also ut in place a mechanism to accurately bill the customer on that basis? |

## 9. Goals- linked

One more way of reducing the risk for the customer is to link the price to tangible business benefits that the customer derives from buying the product or service. This pricing strategy not only requires the ability to take a higher risk but also requires a deep understanding of the customer's business.

The customer's reasons for buying the product or service can be identified amongst a select few, form the business perspective. The customers buy for reducing risk, ensuring compliance, increasing sales, reducing costs or enhancing profits. If you can identify the contribution your product or service makes to one or more of these business goals, and price the product based on quantification of benefits delivered by achieving these goals, the probability of the customer buying your product or service goes up.

A few examples of linking price of a business solution to customer's business goals in a business-to-business context are given below.

| ***Business Goal*** | ***Measurement*** | ***Price*** |
|---|---|---|
| Reduce credit risk | Percentage of bad debts | 10% of the amount the reduction in bad debts |
| Improved compliance | Improved employee score on an understanding of data security | 5% premium on base price for 10% improvement in score |

| *Business Goal* | *Measurement* | *Price* |
|---|---|---|
| Sales | Improved conversion ratio | 5% of sales to customers from an increase in conversion ratio above 20% |
| Costs | Reduced cost of rectifying defects | Rs 50 each for a reduction in returns caused by a product defect |
| Profits | Improvement in profit margin | 15% of the increase in gross margin from delivery of the service |

It is also possible to set goals, measurements and metrics for a product sold to the end consumer and price the product accordingly. The purpose of a person buying car insurance, home insurance or a household item's insurance is to cover the risk from damage or loss. The probability of loss would be lower in case the vehicle is parked in a covered basement, or a locked garage. Likewise, the possibility of damage or theft is lower when the vehicle is fitted with the anti-theft gadget. The likelihood of damage to house property is higher in case there is a restaurant in the premises where cooking gas is used, or there is a petrol pump next door. The possibility of theft of household items is less when the anti-burglar alarm is fitted in the home. The insurance companies charge a lower or higher premium based on such variables to link the price (premium) to the customer goals.

## *Goals- linked pricing - Checklist*

| | |
|---|---|
| 1 | Are you able to identify customer's business goals that are directly impacted by your product or service? |
| 2 | Are you able to identify metrics to measure performance against customer's business goals, measure the results and demonstrate usefulness to the customer? |
| 3 | Will the linking of price to the achievement of customer's business goals increase conversions enough to compensate for the risk of lower realization of the goals are not achieved? |
| 4 | Do you have a mechanism in place to analyse the impact of the goals- linked pricing strategy and offer the linkage such that the profits are maximized while ensuring customer satisfaction? |

## Comparison of risk-reward based Strategies

The table below compares various risk- reward-based strategies.

| *Criteria* | Risk for vendor | Risk for customer | Usage in Projects pricing | Usage in Products pricing | Usage in Services pricing | Usage in the B2B market | Usage in the B2C market |
|---|---|---|---|---|---|---|---|
| *One-time license* | Medium | Medium | Low | Medium | Low | Medium | Medium |
| *License & Renewal* | Low | Medium | Low | Medium | Low | High | High |
| *Free trial* | High | Low | Low | Medium | Low | Medium | High |
| *ROI based* | Medium | Low | Medium | High | High | High | Low |
| *Pricing for product co-creation* | Low | Low | Medium | High | Low | High | Low |
| *Pricing for product validation* | Medium | Low | Low | High | Medium | High | Low |
| *Money-Back Guarantee* | High | Low | Low | High | Medium | Medium | High |
| *Transaction based* | High | Medium | Low | High | Low | High | Medium |
| *Goals-linked* | High | Low | Medium | Medium | Medium | High | Low |

*"Prices are ultimately set by value, not by the competition or supply/demand, but by value."*

***—Ron Baker***

# CHAPTER *Twelve*

## *Innovative Strategies of Pricing*

*"The show is not selling, let's raise prices!"*

***—Ronda Helton***

We classified pricing strategies into 5 broad categories – traditional, sales-driven, modern, risk-reward based and innovative. The innovative strategy has evolved recently with services contributing a larger share of jobs and growth in developed and developing economies. Services marketing needs more innovative strategy since they are intangible. Technology products, including online and mobile app-driven businesses extensively adopted new strategies since their business model itself is a big change from the manufacturing-driven business models.

Apart from other marketing aspects, the way the new economy businesses price the products is a fundamental shift in the way the art and science of pricing worked in the past. Let's look at the advantages and limitations of following innovative pricing strategies.

## Advantages of innovative pricing strategies

1. Well-suited for services and technology businesses
2. Higher scope of cross-learning and adaptation
3. In tune with the fast-changing business models
4. Provide more options to customers

5. Encourage creativity from product design to usage
6. Establishes linkages between price and value

## Limitations of innovative pricing strategies

1. Legal and ethical challenges around data privacy
2. Limit options for customers by creating monopolies
3. Require extensive expertise in pricing
4. Require capabilities in financial modelling and data analysis
5. Require continuous experimentation to manage risks
6. Requires in-depth knowledge of customer's business and industry trends

## Innovative pricing strategies

Some of the key innovative pricing strategies include

1. Customer as a data
2. Click & Mortar
3. Pricing a niche
4. Modular vs enterprise
5. Choice/ Anchoring/ Decoy
6. Yes/ No pricing
7. Dynamic
8. Funnel pricing / Zero price

9. Pre-selling
10. Pay – as – you – wish
11. Cannibalisation/ Price skimming
12. Freemium/ Subscription (SaaS/PaaS)

Let's look at the risk-rewards based pricing strategies one by one.

## 1. Customer as a data

*"If you are not paying for it, you are the product."*

***—Panagiotis Papadopoulos***

One of the biggest stories of this millennia is the rise of internet-driven businesses like Google, Facebook, Twitter and Instagram. They have grown from being a start-up to virtual monopolies in their own space, in last approx. 15 years. Google's share of worldwide desktop search engines is around 88%, with the next competitor's share at less than 5% (Reference 1)

Facebook had a massive 70% market share in social networking space, which is now reduced to ~37%, with a rise in the market share of microblogging sites Twitter and Reddit. Facebook still has close to 2.2 billion monthly active users. (Reference 2) WhatsApp, with 1.6 billion users globally, has a most prominent share of the instant messaging apps. (Reference 3)

One commonality across these platforms is that they do not charge anything to the users. The access to the platform, whether over the web or through an app, posting or viewing content, downloading user data and such features are available for free. This, coupled with their usability and networking effect, has attracted billions of users to these platforms.

As Dan Ariely mentions in his book, "Predictably Irrational - The Hidden Forces That Shape Our Decisions", "Zero is not just another price, it turns out. Zero is an emotional hot button—a source of irrational excitement.". The fundamental reason is that at zero, a customer doesn't see a downside to 'buying' the product. We are afraid of making a wrong decision. At zero, we are not scared of making a wrong decision, because we perceive we have nothing to lose (no downside). People don't mind spending their most valuable asset, time, when they get something for free, e.g., wait a long time in the queue to visit a museum for free on a Sunday.

The users are attracted to use these websites or apps precisely because they do not see any downside of using those. Even a small price will force the users to question the utility.

The users, or the customers, themselves are a 'product', which these websites sell to the advertisers. The advertisers are willing to pay huge money for this data since they get tools that help them design targeted marketing campaigns that improve conversions. The technology has also enabled tracking the user behaviour and response to the advertisements, thus enhancing its appeal.

The customer as a product is not in itself a new strategy though. Most mainstream media companies sell newspapers and magazines at a loss and make money from the advertisements. The new-age digital enterprises implemented this strategy better, faster and on a larger scale.

***Customer as a data pricing - Checklist***

| | |
|---|---|
| 1 | Does any of your products provide scope for offering the product for free and later monetising the data you collect from the customers? |
| 2 | Are there any regulatory constraints on using customer data? If yes, do you make necessary policy disclosures and ensure that the data privacy laws are fully complied with? |
| 3 | Is the free pricing helpful in generating volumes that will compensate for the loss in revenue through alternate sources? |
| 4 | Is the profile of the product customers (users) such that the third- parties will be willing to pay for access to the data? |

## 2. Click & Mortar

For centuries, the location of the business decided where its sales would come from. The goods had to be carried to and stored near the place where they were to be consumed. With the advent of cheaper and universally accessible technologies, businesses could target customers everywhere. This change occurred around 1960s, and after 1990s, with eCommerce it gained momentum.

Ecommerce pioneers like Amazon and eBay led the eCommerce revolution and gained considerable market reach in the last two decades. This posed significant challenges to small retailers as well as retail chains. The eCommerce players grew by expanding the market and to a certain extent, by cannibalising the sales of the retailers. Innovation like delivering books in the electronic platform (such as Amazon Kindle) or selling product key for software products like Microsoft Office online cannibalised the retailer's business.

Once the necessity of selling goods and services online was realised, many retail businesses took their business online in addition to running physical stores. Most recently, eCommerce giants like Amazon are setting up physical stores. Currently, Amazon has four forms of physical retail stores, viz., Amazon books, Amazon 4-star, Amazon Go, and Amazon pop-up, for selling books, devices, merchandise, and food. Other eCommerce players like Alibaba and JD.com have physical retail stores as well. eBay is also trying out the concept, and my go for these after initial results are positive. Big retailers like Walmart, Kmart and Croma have built a considerable online presence.

*"With the advent of the internet, customers can compare prices easily, and this has raised the importance of pricing among the 4Ps. That being said, branding is still crucial. Customers will not necessarily go for the cheapest*

*brand. However, they are more than likely to buy their preferred brand from the retailer offering the lowest price."*

***—Philip Kotler***

The click-and-mortar, i.e., online plus offline, presence, creates a new challenge in pricing. The customers can now view the prices online, compare them with the competitor's prices online, and then decide whether to visit the physical store. Additionally, the customers in the store can compare the competitor's prices while inside the store.

The success of this business model, therefore, requires that the prices offered are comparable to the prices offered by the competitors online, and that the stores salespersons are trained to cross-sell and up-sell other more profitable products when the customer walks in for buying the product in-store. The salespersons are also being authorised to offer the prices offered by the competitors online, within a certain range, to close the deal. In-store offers such as discounts on related products, discount coupons, additional warranties and membership discounts are deployed to increase conversions from footfalls. One more strategy is to introduce more "store brands", i.e., products procured "white-label" and sold under its own brand. These can drive sales at high margin due to secure buying, lower cost of storage and carrying the inventory and opportunity to leverage salesperson's skills in-tore.

Besides retailers, many retail businesses such as restaurants, pharmacies, newspapers, magazines and groceries are now successfully leveraging click-and-mortar business model and pricing strategies, using aggregator apps.

The services businesses are using a modified version of click-and-mortar strategy by delivering services over the internet. The lawyers, coaches, consultants and other advisors provide their services over the internet at a lower cost because it saves their time. They can, additionally use the latest web meting tools to deliver their services to a group of customers which helps reduce the price for an individual customer, while increasing the profitability for the service provider. The services offered onsite or from their premises are charged a higher rate (fees).

***Click and Mortar pricing - Checklist***

| | |
|---|---|
| 1 | Have you analysed the costs of adding an online/ physical presence to your current model of selling through physical/ online presence? |
| 2 | Have you investigated the potential cannibalisation of revenue from online/ physical presence by revenue generated by using click- and – mortar model? |
| 3 | Have you analysed the impact of competitor's pricing strategies because of graduating to the tick- and – mortar presence? |
| 4 | Does your product catalogues provide opportunities for cross-selling and up-selling through click- and – mortar presence? |

## 3. Pricing a niche

Most businesses start with a niche offering. That is, they begin with offering select products and services, and focus on delivering value, on growing in that niche. When you offer products in a niche, you are naturally targeting a tiny section of the market to whom those products have an appeal. That's the reason; most businesses tend to broaden their products and services portfolio beyond the niche, to appeal to a more extensive customer base.

Some of the businesses continue to focus on a niche as a strategy because of certain advantages of being in a niche market. There are relatively less focused competitors. The level of expertise developed by working in a niche is also high. Therefore, the pricing of a niche offering also requires special attention.

The players who operate in a niche, with their deep insights, should carve out multiple offerings within a niche to target a broader market without moving away from a niche position. An example of a strategy that a consulting firm can use for developing a niche offering and pricing those offerings is given on next page.

One of the ways of tapping into the higher revenues from a larger target market is to offer other products and services under a different brand and position them accordingly. Several companies have successfully executed this strategy.

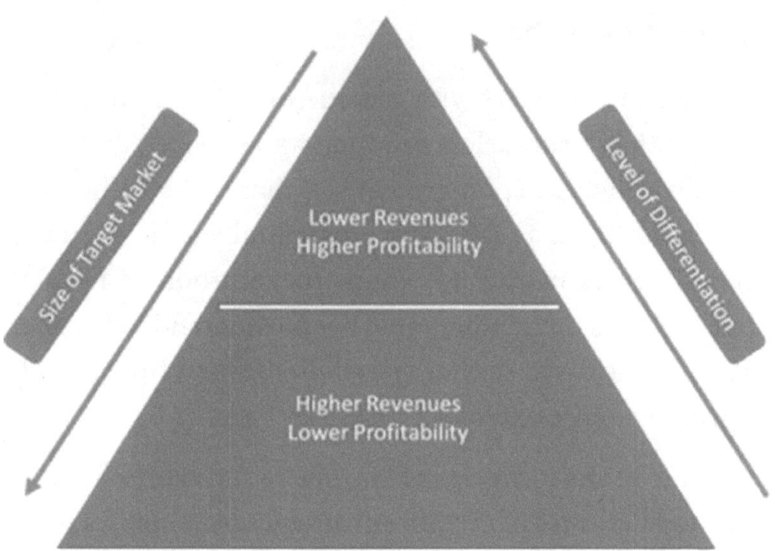


### *Pricing a niche- Checklist*

| | |
|---|---|
| 1 | Have you analysed the pros and cons of focusing on a niche versus positioning as a generic product/services provider with potentially higher target customers? |
| 2 | Have you developed a set of offerings that help you leverage your expertise and focus on a niche segment? |
| 3 | Do you have a clear idea of which segment each offering targets and the value delivered to that target segment? |
| 4 | Does the portfolio of offerings lead to more significant customer base, higher revenues and profitability, and potential for cross-selling ad up-sell? |
| 5 | Are you able to measure and track the profitability across all offerings within the niche? |

## 4. Modular vs enterprise

This strategy has been very effectively used by the Enterprise applications providers like SAP, Oracle and others over the last decade or so. It is relevant for other industries as well.

The customer may be happy with your product but may still hesitate to buy for reasons such as he is not sure whether he needs the full functionality. Also, he may be happy with the product he is currently using and not want to replace it and take additional efforts, money and risk involved in moving over.

The product design should, therefore, be 'modular', i.e., the components should work stand alone as well. The necessary interfaces that support working with other elements, not necessarily from the same seller, should be designed and developed. The components should use a standard base product with master data or configurations that are leveraged across the segments.

Modular pricing will attract customers who are looking for a price which fits their needs and not something which offers more. The modules will, therefore, be individually priced to work out cheaper. The prices for the individual modules will, however, add up much more than the enterprise price.

The enterprise applications players have, with modular pricing, been able to open up market of those companies who don't need full enterprise application. Customers who provide platform-based services, such as payroll services providers, subscribe to the modules and use those, instead of full enterprise product, which doesn't make business sense.

Modular design and pricing also help in developing higher expertise and rich functionality within the niche, hire, train and retain talent, and stand out from the competition.

***Modular vs enterprise pricing - Checklist***

| | |
|---|---|
| 1 | Have you explored the possibility of taking a modular approach to the product development? |
| 2 | Are the individual modules designed to deliver distinct functionality and business benefits? |
| 3 | Do the modules work seamlessly with each other to provide full enterprise functionality in case the customer needs it? |
| 4 | Have you analysed business benefits and costs to work out the ROI for the customers at the modular level as well as the enterprise level? |
| 5 | Have you designed and developed the modules such that they easily integrate with other products in the customer's business environment? |

## 5. Choice/ Anchoring/ Decoy

Customers need a choice. They may know their needs well, agree that the product solves their problem, and thus have a good reason to buy. However, if there is no reference scale, most customers find it difficult to decide.

In case the product doesn't provide that reference scale, the customer will look for the reference scale elsewhere, which means getting a competitor in the picture.

Once the competition is in the picture, the customer gets an altogether different scale to compare with. The competitor may present the product features and benefits in an entirely different way, which makes the comparison confusing and complicated. It is difficult to compare Apple products with other competing products because the entire approach of presenting features is different.

If the customer can't find a competing product to compare with, he may postpone the decision to buy. This is a situation you would want to avoid. Hence it is imperative that you provide a choice to the customers. Too many options will confuse the customer. Therefore, it is generally considered that providing three variants is the optimum choice, and anything more than five is avoidable.

While presenting the choices, the 'anchoring' technique is frequently used by the organisations. The variant or option which sets the 'anchor' in the mind of the customer is the one that has the best possible value at the highest possible price. The other two variants are priced lower and provide lower cost. The customer can see that the most top-priced option has maximum features and benefits, though priced higher. He may go for that option if it fits his budget. In usual circumstances, he will otherwise go looking for competing options. Still, when you provide other choices by having different variants, he will evaluate those variants against the highest priced option.

Once the scale of reference in the customer's mind is set at a very high price, it is easier to convince the customer that the next best option is better in terms of value, when price is brought into the picture. Let's see an example of the "anchoring".

| Features | Platinum Plan | Gold Plan | Silver Plan |
|---|---|---|---|
| Connect your own domain | √ | √ | √ |
| Remove website Ads | √ | √ | √ |
| Get a 1 year free domain voucher (yearly plans only) | √ | √ | √ |
| Free storage | 20 GB | 10 GB | 2 GB |
| Allocated bandwidth | Unlimited | Unlimited | 2 GB |
| Video upload | 5 hours | 2 hours | - |
| Get credit vouchers and Premium Apps (yearly plans only) | √ | √ | - |
| Get a professional logo and social media logo files | √ | √ | - |
| Receive priority VIP support | √ | - | - |
| Monthly Subscription Price $ payable in advance | 15.00 | 10.00 | 5.00 |
| Annaul Subcription Price $ payable in advance | 150.00 | 100.00 | 50.00 |
| Annaul Subcription Discount | 16.67% | 16.67% | 16.67% |

The platinum plan is best suited for a user who knows what he wants and needs more storage space, uses videos and desires a priority support for configuring website and ensuring quick response to resolve problems faced.

The silver plan has all the essential features that a new user can manage with. All the functionality is pre-built, hence attracting new users with basic features ensures you are not leaving out customers who will look for an upgrade in the future.

Gold Plan is for someone who won't make too many changes after the initial website configuration ad can, therefore, manage without VIP support. Someone who needs. Usually, Gold plan will be marked as "most popular" by suing a popular colour and larger font size.

A user evaluating the plan who would have otherwise thought of Gold plan as very costly will compare with the Gold plan and features with the Silver and Platinum plans and is likely to settle for Gold since now the price 'anchor' is set at $ 150. The website suggests that the Gold Plan is "most popular". The Gold plan is desired to be the leader and Platinum Plan a "decoy" to set the "anchor" high.

*"Pricing decisions do not always have to be about raising or lowering prices from their current levels. They can also be about making price offers in different, creative ways, where the customer perceives that the value provided by the company has increased significantly, even when actual prices have not changed or gone up."*

***—Utpal Dholakia***

The anchoring is a most widely used strategy in selling technology-driven products and services. It has a sound base in theory as well.

The strategy and configuration for 'anchoring' price for maximising revenue and optimising profitability are depicted below. The segregation of features into essential, value and premium features requires a good understanding of customer needs and perception.

| Strategy & Configuration | Platinum | Gold | Silver |
|---|---|---|---|
| Target % of total unit sales | 10% | 70% | 20% |
| Target % of total revenue | 20% | 70% | 10% |
| Target Net Margin | 50% | 30% | 15% |
| Essential features | Included | Included | Included |
| Value features | Included | Included | - |
| Premium features | Included | - | - |

## *Choice/ Anchoring/ Decoy pricing - Checklist*

| | |
|---|---|
| 1 | Is creating variants or versions of a product a part of your product designing process, and is it also a key performance indicator for the team? |
| 2 | Are the variants or versions created after carefully analysing product features and benefits that appeal to different customers within the target customer base? |
| 3 | Have you created adequately differentiated variants and priced them according to the purchasing power and expectations of the customers? |
| 4 | Have you ensured that the customers get enough choice (say, 3 variants) and at the same time, are not confused by presenting with too many variants (say, less than 5)? |
| 5 | Have you identified the product variant that delivers the best possible value to the segment of the customers who form a significant part of the target customer base? |
| 6 | Is the price for the different versions of the product set such that a convincing but high enough anchor is set in the minds of the customers? |

| | |
|---|---|
| 7 | Are the customers able to distinguish between the variants, their benefits and compare the prices across version, to make an intelligent decision quickly regarding the version they would like to buy? |
| 8 | Do you have a mechanism to track the highest-selling version, the reasons for customer's choice, customer's feedback after usage, and impact on the conversions? |

## 6. Yes/ No Pricing

Yes/ No pricing is a strategy of providing a binary choice to the prospect, instead of coming up with options. The intent is only to take on those customers who are worth working with, at that point in time.

Yes/ No pricing strategy is of use in those industries where there is a capacity constraint that can't be immediately resolved. E.g., a consulting firm has a bandwidth constraint due to a number of experts who can deliver consulting engagement. In this situation is they get an inquiry from a prospect whose lifetime value is not perceived to be high, they may quote a premium price to the customer. This price could be way higher than the usual price they quote to other customers who are perceived to have a high lifetime value.

If the customer in question is willing to pay the premium price, because of high profitability on that deal itself, it makes sense taking up that customer. Otherwise, losing that business has a shallow impact, since the delivery capacity constraint exists anyway.

Even if the prospect refuses to accept the premium price, the price is anchored high with the prospect. If the prospect comes back next time, that high anchor may help negotiate a higher price. Likewise, this is also an opportunity to test a premium pricing strategy and send a signal to the market about changed positioning. The strategy should, however, be used carefully to avoid leaving a bad experience with the prospect. This strategy is opposite of providing a choice to the customers to get a widen the customer base.

***Yes/ No pricing - Checklist***

| | |
|---|---|
| 1 | Do you face capacity constraints that make it difficult to the peak demand without comprising on the quality and taking a higher level of risk? |
| 2 | Do you want to set a higher anchor price for your offerings and explore customer's feedback for the top anchor? |
| 3 | Are you prepared for letting the customer go rather than deliver under constraint and with higher risk? |
| 4 | Are you prepared to deliver to the customer who buys at a high anchor and ensure customer satisfaction? |

## 7. Dynamic

Dynamic pricing is a pricing strategy that tries to maximise the revenues and profits by constantly analysing the demand and supply patterns.

At the peak demand, the business has an opportunity to price the product higher. In case the supply is limited unless the prices are increased, there is a notional loss of potential revenue and profitability. One of the ways of partially or fully avoiding this notional loss is to charge a higher price when the demand peaks, a strategy often called 'surge pricing'.

The customer who has an acute need for the product or service will be willing to pay the higher price. The one who can manage without the product or service will wait for the price to go down. The supplier profits from surge price during peak demand times and has an opportunity to pass on the benefit to the other customers when the demand is lower.

The dynamic pricing is being used in various industries, ranging from airlines, taxis, hotels and electricity manufacturing or distribution companies. One common feature of these industries is that their product is 'perishable'. That is, an airline seat, if empty, generates zero revenue, and that revenue is lost forever. A cab driver and the cab, both, are unutilised, if there is no passenger. A hotel room, if not occupied, is an example of room-tariff revenue lost forever. While it is possible to store the electricity, the cost of storage, comprising of investment in storage equipment and loss in storage, is very high.

On the other hand, the demand for these products and services changes dynamically. The cabs typically experience peak demand during morning and evening. The airlines experience peak demand on certain days and times. The hotels in cities that have demand from business travellers, experience demand on weekdays, and the occupancy goes down considerably over the weekends (Friday, Saturday and Sunday nights). The hotels at tourist destinations like hill-stations, experience peak demand during school holidays and weekends, whereas the occupancy rates go down considerably during the weekdays and non-holiday season.

Higher tariff during peak demand times helps these industries maximise profits, and lower tariff during non-peak demand times helps them attract customers. The non-peak prices may be set using cost-plus, or marginal pricing strategies explained elsewhere.

The dynamic pricing is being used in a few other industries as well. The movies, dramas and performances are priced higher in some theatres during the initial weeks. One of the leading soft-drink brands toyed with the idea of pricing their soft drinks higher at the vending machines when the temperature. The tolls on the inner-city roads and the parking tickets and passes are priced based on the demand. E.g., Parking passes in commercial zones are priced way higher than those in residential zones.

With the emergence of machine learning, artificial intelligence and predictive analytics, dynamic pricing will find applicability in more industries where massive data is available for analysis and back-testing. The new algorithms analyse not only the firm's demand and supply patterns but also the competitor's pricing, to come up with intelligent dynamic pricing.

***Dynamic pricing - Checklist***

| | |
|---|---|
| 1 | Do you have a system in place to continuously assess the demand and supply for your products and services? |
| 2 | Have you evaluated the price elasticity of demand for your products and services to develop upper and lower range within which the price should be set? |
| 3 | Have you developed a dynamic pricing model that quickly decides the price and cascades the same to various channels? |
| 4 | Do you have necessary tools and skills to leverage latest technological advances in data analytics, big data, machine learning and artificial intelligence to constantly improve on the dynamic pricing model to optimise revenues and profitability? |
| 5 | Have you factored in regulatory constraints in dynamically setting the prices for your products and services? |
| 6 | Do you have a mechanism to analyse customer satisfaction levels in the light of dynamic prices? |

## 8. Funnel pricing / Zero price

The classic marketing funnel, though criticised often, survives with adaptations in various forms. It has been improvised for the digital economy, use of content marketing, the evolution of eCommerce and the rise of Software as a Service (SaaS) and Platform as a Service (PaaS) delivery models. The conversion ratios from one stage to the next are tracked more rigorously for allocating marketing dollars.

While developing the funnel, testing it through experimentation and implementing the funnel, pricing cannot be ignored. A funnel that gets high leads at the top end, and progressively moves the customer through a journey of a first-time customer, a repeat buyer to a loyal customer, should map products, variants and price to the customer needs.

| Product/ Service | Benefits/ Deliverables | Price | Trust Level | Money Risk | Time Risk | Conversion % |
|---|---|---|---|---|---|---|
| Basic | Medium | Low | Low | Low | Low | |
| Value | Medium | Low | Medium | Low | Medium | |
| Value | High | Medium | Medium | Medium | Medium | |
| Premium | Very High | High | High | High | High | |

The products and services portfolio should be designed to get the first-time customers to sign-up at a low price, since at that stage, they have low trust levels, and would like to take low money risk and time-risk with you, i.e., invest less time. However, the products and services at this stage should deliver a value which exceeds the expectations of the customer whose expectation is aligned to the primary product.

Once the customers experience the value delivered at low risk of time and money, they would be happy to invest in progressively buying buy higher-value products and services. It is essential, however, that at every stage through the funnel, you must deliver as much value to the customer as possible. The funnel is not designed to "trap" the customer through false assurances; it is designed to take the customer through a journey where he progressively takes higher risk with you, because he trusts you more.

Efforts on selling a premium product or service to a new customer will not yield results because there is a low probability of success. If you appropriately position your products across the customer acquisition funnel, your chances of conversion of a prospect into a customer will be higher at every stage. As a corollary, the cost of customer acquisition will be lower.

***Funnel pricing/ zero price - Checklist***

| | |
|---|---|
| 1 | Have you analysed the customer's time-risk in the price -risk of buying your various products and services and mapped those to the trust level? |
| 2 | Have you created a portfolio of products and services that the target customers need? |
| 3 | Have you created products with differentiated value delivered, time and money risk involved, and mapped those with the customer journey? |
| 4 | Have you designed a strategy to up-sell higher value (bigger ticket size) offerings at each stage of the funnel, as the customer develops trust, and the time risk and money risk goes down? |
| 5 | Have you allocated the budget to deliver value at each stage at lower profitability (or zero profitability or loss)? |

| | |
|---|---|
| 6 | Have you assigned a target conversion ratio as you move along the funnel, and continuously measure actual conversions, to change the pricing as you go along? |

## 9. Pre-selling

The pre-selling strategy involves marketing and pricing a product before it arrives in the market. This strategy is popular in marketing some of the products such as movies, TV serials and books.

The movie screening rights as well as the right to the merchandise are sold to the distributors and merchandise manufacturers or sellers ahead of the movie screening, or, in many cases, ahead of the production. The TV serial producers put together a tentative production idea, including the plot, the scriptwriter, key actors etc and come up with approximate costs of production. They take this idea to the TV channels who assess the potential viewership and allocate the budget and decide on the possible time slots. The budget is key for the producer to start the production and the time slot is critical for the advertisers to indicate the budgets they are willing to allocate on behalf of the brands who may want to advertise. The main sponsor who funds most cost takes the decision based on the theme of the serial as well as the profile of the audience, which is likely to watch the serial.

The books are pre-sold ahead of fully finishing the book. If you are not a well-known author, the people who buy the book before it gets published are likely to be close friends, family members, and business associate. If you are known expert in the area, which is the topic of the book, some people will buy based on your reputation as well. This is usually relevant for the non-fiction category of books. In the fiction category, pre-selling is a bit of a challenge. The pre-selling of a fiction works between an author who is well-known and a publishing house which believes they will be able to leverage the past track record of the author to market the book. The royalties that famous authors command from the publishers even before writing the book can be substantial.

*"Don't sell yourself short. No one will value you. Set a fair price for you, your book, your services, whatever it is that you have to offer. Most of us set way too low a price. Put it a little higher than you would normally be inclined to do. The worst that can happen is someone will come along and steal it."*

***—John Kremer***

The buy who buys the product before being ready takes more risk than otherwise, with the hope of making more profits. The seller covers the risk of the product not selling after production and losing the money spent in production. Thus, the risk is partially passed on from the producer to the marketer (film distributors, merchandise producers, TV channels or book publishers).

***Pre-selling - Checklist***

| | |
|---|---|
| 1 | Do you enjoy enough brand equity based on past performance such that you will be able to pre-sell the product before creation? |
| 2 | Have you set the minimum pre-selling target that you would want to achieve before the end of the pre-launch offer? |
| 3 | Have you priced the pre-selling offer such that the customers see the apparent benefit of taking a higher risk? |
| 4 | Do you have a strategy in place to leverage the customers whom you have acquired through pre-selling, for selling after the formal product launch? |

## 10. Pay – as – you – wish

Pas-as-you-wish (PAYW) or Pay-what-you-want (PWYW) is a rarely used strategy in those industries where the product or a service has a universal appeal.

A south Indian restaurant chain used this strategy for initial few months from opening in Singapore and Australia to attract customers who had not experienced that restaurant in southern India. They went back to the usual pricing after those few months. Interestingly, almost all the customers paid for the food by benchmarking with another restaurant in that city which served couth Indian meals. This strategy has also been tried by the charities which helped food in areas with poor or destitute populations in the USA and other countries. However, in many cases, the brands which attempted to run this strategy for long had to close down due to losses over some time.

This strategy has been used by museums where they asked the visitors to donate any amount as they felt like while leaving the museum. It is difficult to price the artefacts that are displayed in the museum, and therefore also difficult to price the experience of visiting the museum. Many museums across the world practice this strategy on select days in the year to attract people who would not otherwise experience the museums. Any money that gets collected as donations is considered a plus.

Theatres have used this strategy while launching dramas and music concerts. This can be a good tactic for launching new artists under a big banner. The risk for the patron is zero, and the theatre has an opportunity to make money if the artists strike a chord with the audience.

Overall experience of this strategy is that the customers pay high if they feel the venture is socially beneficial. The amount that the customer pays is dependent on the peer norms since this strategy appeals to social feelings. This strategy is good for launches and promotions, and for penetration into a market since it involves zero risk for the customer.

This strategy also offers the advantage of price discrimination, i.e., the customer can pay higher or lower price depending on the perceived value and his ability to pay. The price paid by the customer can additionally be anchored around a certain number by displaying a base price, suggested price, or in some cases indicative cost of producing the product or delivering the service. Most customers are observed to pay near or above these benchmarks.

This strategy looks very similar to the no-questions-asked money-back policy. However, this strategy works better in some cases since the customer doesn't have to decide until after experiencing the product, hence the chances of conversion are high. Also, the cost of collecting and repaying money is avoided. The market in which this strategy is used should be carefully analysed in advance to ensure freeloaders don't land up to experience the product without any intention of paying whatsoever.

***Pay- as -You – Wish (PAYW) pricing - checklist***

| | |
|---|---|
| 1 | Do you have a mechanism in place to qualify the customers who avail the PAYW based on their potential need for the product and ability to pay the price at the high end of the range, i.e., mechanism to avoid the freeloaders? |
| 2 | Have you tested the product for quality and are confident that most of the customers will pay the minimum price at which the comparable products are usually priced? |
| 3 | Have you created a scenario with the distribution of the customer across the price range, and have a system in place to estimate and compare the customers who paid the price across the price range? |

| | |
|---|---|
| 4 | Do you have the capacity to absorb the potential losses from the PAYW pricing strategy if the customers do not pay as estimated in advance? |
| 5 | Does the product or a service immediately provide the customer an idea of how satisfied he is, with the product? |
| 6 | Have you explored and decided on using an anchor by displaying a base price, a suggested price or a cost of production of the product? |
| 7 | Does the product have a high frequency of purchase, yielding a high lifetime value of the customer? |

## 11. Cannibalisation/ Price skimming

Product cannibalisation is the adverse impact of sales of the old product because of the introduction of a new product that provides additional features in addition to the one which is replaced. The original product is thus a better version of the old one. A product which is cannibalised experiences reduced sales and may over time become obsolete.

The companies that manage their product lifecycle are well aware of the threat of cannibalisation of their existing products. So much so, they make efforts to see that they introduce a new product that cannibalises the old one, instead of a competitor introducing the new product. This ensures that they maintain the leadership position in the market as the technology and the product keeps evolving.

Since the new product is technologically advanced and provides more features and benefits, there is a scope for charging higher price. The successful cannibalisation strategy involves introducing the new product such that the customer develops the scarcity mindset and is therefore willing to pay a premium price for the new product.

In some cases, the price of the old product may have to be reduced to keep its sales from nosediving. However, the strategy is managed such that the new product is sold at a considerably higher price. In contrast, the price of the old product's price is reduced only marginally, or not reduced at all. The former product continues to attract buyers who typically prefer 'stable' version of the product and are averse to experimentation. It is feasible to charge higher price for the new product because it generally appeals to the "early adopters" who desire new, exclusive features, and like to experiment with those. Creating a scarcity mindset by launching a limited number initially and creating a charged atmosphere, like Apple does for a new version of its iPhone, can reap high rewards from premium pricing.

This strategy is prevalent in a product-driven by technology that target an affluent section of the population. The higher price of the new version of the product is justifiable to this target because of the new "enhance" features and benefits. Even when the old version is reduced in price, it is reduced by a small fraction and soon discontinued not to allow cannibalisation of sales of the newer products.

***Cannibalisation/ Price Skilling pricing - Checklist***

| | |
|---|---|
| 1 | Have you estimated the impact of introduction of a new product variant on the current variant of the product, i.e., cannibalisation rate? |
| 2 | Does it make sense introducing the latest variant of the product at the cost of cannibalisation of the current product? |
| 3 | Is there an opportunity for using price skimming for clearing the inventory of the existing product variant? |
| 4 | Have you worked out the possibility of the customer moving to a competitor product due to price skimming, and if yes, is it within an acceptable range? |
| 5 | Are you able to charge a premium price for the latest product variant, that is justified by the additional customer benefits delivered from the improvements? |
| 6 | Are you ready to appropriately target the early adopters for the new premium product, while retaining the customers who are averse to experimentation? |

## 12. Freemium/ Subscription (SaaS/PaaS)

One of the biggest changes in information technology in this decade has been the rise and dominance of social media, mobility, analytics and cloud technologies, popularly known as SMAC technology stack. The usage of mobility, analytics and cloud technology for building business and consumer technology applications made it possible for the vendors to use innovative pricing strategies for these applications.

The Software as a Service (SaaS) and Platform as a Service (PaaS) delivery models involve building applications that are hosted on the cloud (public cloud in most cases, and private cloud in some cases). These applications typically deliver standardised best-in-class functionality, provide ease of configuration, provide data migration tools that make implementation easier, are delivered over the internet and are user-friendly. In-built tools for reporting and analytics handle most of the user-specific needs that would otherwise call for a customer-specific customisation.

The pricing of these SaaS and PaaS applications typically zero or negligible upfront investment. This reduces the money-risk considerably for the customer. The ease of configuration and migration also reduced the time-risk of the customer significantly. The customer pays for the user through a subscription model, which involves monthly or yearly plans. The basis for pricing is also flexible to accommodate a customer who uses limited functionality (using modular pricing) and runs a small business (using user-based pricing).

The scalability of the applications is based primarily on design and architecture. If these are architected for large volumes and throughput, the storage of extensive data doesn't pose a challenge, since cloud technology is extensible.

These products are frequently released in 'light' mode with limited functionality, which is offered using 'freemium' strategy. The freemium strategy involved providing a limited functionality the product for unlimited period of use to convince the customer about the benefits of the product and also get the customer used to the product and make it difficult to move to a competitor's product.

The customer may stay a freemium subscriber forever using the limited functionality. Special offers are made at frequent intervals to the freemium subscriber to move to be a paid subscription which gives much rich functionality of the product. Freemium is, thus, a strategy to keep competitors at bay while increasing the chances of conversion to a paid subscriber.

The technology vendors who successfully use this pricing strategy have grown fast and can maintain or increase profitability. However, this strategy has limited application in legacy industries.

***Freemium/ Subscription (SaaS/ PaaS) pricing - Checklist***

| | |
|---|---|
| 1 | Is your product suitable for the subscription model, i.e., is built once, is scalable enough to be delivered to a large number of customers, without high incremental cost of delivery? |
| 2 | Have you designed and developed a 'light' version of the product with limited but valuable functionality for a freemium user? |
| 3 | Does the freemium subscription product version have enough functionality to develop stickiness and make it difficult for the customer to move to a competitor's product? |

| | |
|---|---|
| 4 | Have you estimated the conversion rates from freemium to paid customers, and created tiered subscription plans to ensure an easier transition? |
| 5 | Is the product design scalable to accommodate a higher number of users without high fixed costs? |
| 6 | Have you aligned a large portion of your costs to the subscription revenues, i.e., ensured most of the costs are aligned to the number of subscribers? |

## Comparison of Innovative Strategies

The table below compares various innovative strategies.

| ***Criteria*** | ***Customer as a data*** | ***Click & Mortar*** | ***Pricing a niche*** | ***Modular vs enterprise*** | ***Choice/ Anchoring/ Decoy*** | ***Yes/ No*** | ***Dynamic*** | ***Funnel pricing / Zero price*** | ***Pre-selling*** | ***Pay – as – you – wish*** | ***Cannibalisation/ Price skimming*** | ***Freemium/ Subscription (SaaS/ PaaS)*** |
|---|---|---|---|---|---|---|---|---|---|---|---|---|
| Risk for vendor | High | Medium | Medium | Medium | Low | Medium | Medium | High | Low | High | Medium | High |
| Risk for customer | Medium | Low | Low | Low | Medium | Low | Medium | Low | High | Low | Low | Low |
| Usage in Projects pricing | Low | Low | Medium | Low | Low | Medium | Medium | Low | Low | Low | Low | Low |
| Usage in Products pricing | High | High | Medium | High | High | Low | Low | Medium | High | Medium | High | Low |
| Usage in Services pricing | High | Medium | High | Low | Medium | High | High | High | Low | Medium | Low | High |
| Usage in the B2B market | Low | Medium | Medium | High | Low | Medium | Medium | Low | Low | Low | Low | High |
| Usage in the B2C market | High | High | High | High | High | High | High | High | High | Medium | High | High |

*"The strategic price you set for your offering must not only attract buyers in large numbers but also help you to retain them."*

—***W. Chan Kim,*** Blue Ocean Strategy, Expanded Edition: How to Create Uncontested Market Space and Make the Competition Irrelevant

***Reference 1***

https://www.statista.com/statistics/216573/worldwide-market-share-of-search-engines/

***Reference 2***

https://www.dreamgrow.com/top-10-social-networking-sites-market-share-of-visits/

***Reference 3***

https://www.messengerpeople.com/global-messenger-usage-statistics/

# CHAPTER *Thirteen*

## *Pricing as a Science and An Art*

*"Successful pricing is an art, not a science."*

***—John I. Leahy***

Is pricing an art, or is it a science? Creative product design and pricing definitely needs artistic bend of mind. The innovative pricing strategies discussed in the previous chapter are a result of a fertile brain-challenging the existing practices and notions and looking for new ways to price the products and services. On the other hand, pricing has a direct impact on growth, revenues, profitability, cash flow, return on investment and business valuation. Measuring these business metrics call for scientific, mathematical and financial skills.

## What distinguishes art from science?

In general terms, art is an expression which is not bound by specific rules. It derives its meaning and value from the artist and his thought process. There are many forms of art, but when we think of a work of art, we generally think of a painting, a sculpture, a drama or a movie.

The science, on the other hand, develops on the discoveries made in the past. The scientists follow a specific set of rules, which could be formulae, a process, a method and such. Scientific discovery is rarely wholly independent of the previous progress in the field. When we think of science, we think mainly of physics, chemistry, biology and the field of mathematics.

Some of the distinctions between science and art can be listed as

1. Science is objective, whereas art is subjective
2. Science advances through observation and experimentation, whereas arts advance through abstract expression
3. Science puts substance ahead of form, whereas arts puts form ahead of substance

## Is pricing a science?

Therefore, let's ask whether pricing is a science. If pricing is a science, there would be a clear-cut method, process or formula for pricing a product or service for growth and profitability. Once that method, process or formula is followed, the results would be accurate as predicted.

We should, therefore, have a formula which tells us the variables to feed, or a method or a process that step-by-step guides us to a price that guarantees the results. This would make decisions simple and ensure growth and profitability.

This is not the case. Pricing, as a specialised field of expertise, has gained traction only recently. There is no predefined formula, method or process. Thus, pricing is not entirely science.

Pricing process, however, has some elements of the scientific method. Pricing involves observation and experimentation. You observe and analyse the industry, customers, products, competition and such other variables, and accordingly price your products. The prices once decided, are not permanent. As you measure, you will change the pricing strategy or the prices, which is experimentation, just like scientists do.

Some of the aspects of pricing are objective. The price itself (expressed in monetary terms) and the financial model built on the pricing strategy are mathematical exercises. If the assumptions are correct, the results will be as predicted. In that sense, there is a scientific rigour in pricing exercise.

Pricing exercise focuses on clear goals, product, variants, targets and such. Therefore, it puts emphasis on substance, viz., financial goals of the business.

## Is pricing an art?

So, is pricing an art? If pricing is art, it would be an expression driven mainly by the artist's skill, thought process and creativity. The people responsible for pricing in the organisation (usually the marketing team) would use their creativity to set price, and the others would implement it.

The pricing exercise would not have quantifiable goals. The goals would be abstract if at all, they are assigned.

The pricing would be subjective and left to the discretion of the salespeople. The sales team would be free to make an offer to the customer to win business.

However, this is not what we observe in practice. Pricing, a part of marketing, is a rigorous exercise. So much so, nowadays, in some of the organisations, the responsibility of pricing is assigned to specialists who have the necessary theoretical and practical experience.

Pricing exercise does involve understanding customer preferences, needs, problems, expectations and buying behaviour which do not have completely objective measurements. Understanding these requires an understanding of customer and how he is likely to reach to the pricing strategy. Therefore, there is a subjective element in pricing decisions.

Pricing requires extensive collaboration between various teams in the organisation, such as product design, marketing and sales, manufacturing, operations, and so on. This collaboration between teams requires leadership skills which are not entirely objective and quantifiable — the risk-taking ability of the organisation and the leadership is not entirely fair.

Hence pricing involves an artistic element of the understanding customer and managing collaboration between various teams, to strategize and implement pricing decisions.

## Is pricing both an art and a science?

Accounting is the process of analysing, recording, classifying and presenting financial information about the business. It has a set of non-negotiable rules, viz., the "golden rules" of accounting. Accountants require specialised knowledge and skills which need years of training. Yet accounting is considered as both science and art. The reason is, beyond the hard rules of accounting, applying them to a specific context and situation requires exercising skill and judgment beyond the routine accounting exercise.

Likewise, pricing is also an art as well as science. As discussed above, pricing involves an artistic element of the understanding customer and managing collaboration between various teams, to strategize and implement pricing decisions. The pricing process, however, involves observation and analysis of the industry, customers, products, competition and such other variables. As you continue to measure, you will change the pricing strategy or the prices, which is an experimentation, just like scientists do.

Pricing can, therefore, be aptly called both an art and a science.

## Who should decide upon the price?

Who precisely should determine the price of an organisation? This question is crucial because we scarcely come across people who are tasked with the responsibility of 'pricing'. In the recent years, roles like chief Risk Officer (CRO) have gained prominence. In line with the evolving banking governance standards set by Basel Committee on Banking Supervision, most central banks have mandated the role of Chief Risk Officer for the banks. They have come out with the guidelines for the appointment of CROs.

There is no equivalent regulation on pricing, and thankfully so! In a free market, pricing exercise should be the prerogative of each business. There are a few exceptions such as pharmaceutical and fertilisers industry.

Pricing decisions are primarily taken by the CXOs (Chief Executive Officer, Chief Finance Officer and Chief Marketing Officer or Chief Sales Officer). In a project-driven organisation, the price varies for each project. Hence Chief Sales Officer drives the pricing, with a veto with the Chief Finance Officer, who will have a say in the minimum floor for the profitability. In a product-driven organisation, the Chief Marketing Officer and the Chief Finance Officer exercises most control on the decision. The CEO, of course, has the final say.

Pricing as a function or expertise is therefore reflected in titles like 'Pricing Analyst', or leadership titles such as 'Pricing Head', 'Pricing Manager' or 'Pricing Director'. In banking, product owner works with others to set the product pricing. In accounting and consulting firms, the pricing expertise is mostly focused on 'transfer pricing' which is a compliance function, rather than strategic.

The pricing expertise is now being valued across industries with the titles of the leaders reflecting that expertise. In view of the importance of pricing, these roles will gain prominence. However, depending on the industry and organisation, the roles will concentrate mostly within finance or marketing functions, reporting into a CFO or a CMO. Every business should develop pricing expertise internally and hire experts when necessary to fill the gaps or leverage their broad industry experience.

## What skills are needed in deciding the price?

The skills required for making sound pricing decisions can be broadly categorised into four categories – marketing, product design, sales and finance. The skills in these four categories are described below. Note that each of these skills is not exclusive to the category under which they are listed, because every role demands certain cross-functional skills, in addition to skills needed for performing any role, such as communication, information technology, teamwork and leadership.

1. Marketing – Positioning, Segmentation, Market research (secondary and primary), competitor analysis, interpersonal skills, communication design, consumer behaviour, statistical research tools, digital marketing, storytelling, advertising, critical thinking, campaign design, data analytics

2. Product design – surveying, requirements gathering, problem-solving, design thinking, design specification, user experience (UX) and user interface (UI), modelling and prototyping, computer-aided design, quality standards and specifications, creativity and imagination, engineering
3. Sales – prospecting, networking, social selling, relationship management, presentation, objection handling, negotiation, influencing, business and commercial acumen, drive and ambition, agreements and contracts, closing
4. Finance – accounting, reporting, financial analysis, financial modelling, costing, spreadsheets, data analysis, numeracy and analytical ability, commercial and legal, direct and indirect taxes, compliance

The other functions in the organisation such as production, human resources, operations and logistics are also vital to successful pricing strategy.

A pricing expert should have deep expertise in some of these areas in addition to the ability to understand and collaborate with others.

*"You know you have priced right when your customers complain—but buy anyway."*

***—John Harrison***

# CHAPTER *Fourteen*

## *Challenges to Pricing*

*"Anyone can sell a Mercedes for the price of a Hyundai."*

***—Larry Best***

Is it easy to charge a higher price? If it was so easy, why doesn't everyone charge as he wishes and makes money?

No, it is not easy to set a price you want and get customers pay that price. But no one ever said it is easy. The fact is that most entrepreneurs are price- takers and not price-setters.

## Being a price-setter

Are you a price-taker or a price-setter? If you are a price-taker today, you must change your mindset and explore how you can become a price- setter. Differentiate your product. Bundle your products or create a bundle of product and service. Integrate backwards or forwards by partnering. Use tiered pricing to cater to different customer preferences. Or, create intellectual property, the best long-standing differentiator. There are various ways of changing your pricing strategy.

If you are resigned to be a price- taker, you destroy value. There will always be some or other competitor who will beat you on the cost; they will reduce the price, and you will also be forced to do likewise. A price- taker will find it difficult to earn decent margins and create investor wealth. When this is clear, why do businesses accept a price set by the market? Let's explore the critical challenges to pricing the products appropriately, which include:

1. Fixed mindset
2. Lack of Confidence
3. Emotional decision- making
4. Limitations in product design
5. Lack of creativity in pricing
6. Lack of expertise in pricing
7. Challenges of premium positioning
8. Growth versus profit binary
9. Threat of competition
10. Culture of freebies

Let's look at these one by one.

## 1. Mindset

The biggest obstacle to moving to be a price-setter is the 'mindset'. When an entrepreneur launches a business, he has innovative ideas about how to create the product better and serve his customers better than the competitor. Most entrepreneurs select their domain because they have prior experience in that domain, or because they are passionate about the product and the needs it meets.

The initial energies are focused on getting the product and finding a customer. The product is usually priced initially based on the feedback of select known customers who are willing to place their faith in the entrepreneur. How the product should be priced weighs least on the mind of the entrepreneur.

As the product gains momentum, the initial strategy broadly stays. The early customers may be offered a substantial discount to bag the deal, which would be reduced or got rid of, but the plan usually doesn't change. Most customers, typically in a business to a business scenario, refer back to the previous deals and prices and expect similar or lower prices. Price, once set, is difficult to change. What is "difficult to change" appears to be impossible to change. Thus, the entrepreneur must convince himself that his product deserves a higher price than earlier one.

## 2. Lack of confidence

Any upward revision in the price meets with the stiff resistance. Surprisingly, the resistance is foremost in the mind of the entrepreneur, next from his sales team, and then from the customers. The entrepreneur has to cross the first two hurdles before even pitching the product at a higher price to the new customer. He must convince himself that the revised price is the right price and it will work, and then convince his sales team. The sales team is bound to resist since their commissions depend on successfully selling the product.

As you start revising the product prices upwards, and pitch to the customers, you will invariably face resistance. You can't raise the prices simply because you want to. You have to articulate the improved product features and benefits delivered to the customers. The customer would always like to buy the product at as low a price as possible and yet expect the best value. It is for you to convince the customer that you are delivering appropriate value in exchange for a proper price.

If a few deals are lost as you pitch at a higher price, it is easy to lose confidence. The win-loss ratio may move to alarming levels. A very high level of confidence is required to sustain and persist.

## 3. Emotional decision-making

The role played by emotions in business decisions is often underrated. The practice of taking crucial business decisions by involving more team members aims at reducing the impact of emotions of an individual decision-maker. However, given the nature of roles that team members play in any group, it is not possible to divorce the emotions entirely from business decisions.

The emotional basis for decision-making is not necessarily flawed. Organisations that are driven by the personality of the founder are more susceptible to make decisions based on the emotions. Large profitable companies like Apple and Virgin group have successfully leveraged the personality and charisma of the founders to create growing and profitable with large market capitalisation.

However, attributing the success of those organisations to the founder's charisma alone would do injustice to the brains at the back, which help validate these decisions. One of the best ways of ensuring that the emotions alone don't drive the business decisions is to measure the impact of the decisions through numbers and using pre-approved benchmarks for selecting the best amongst the choices.

Pricing decisions are critical to the organisation. Hence, they must be validated using pre-defined benchmarks and their effect fully simulated.

## 4. Limitations in product design

The product design process starts with understanding the customer pain points. The definition of the customer needs is very critical to the design and forms basis of subsequent brainstorming to come up with options and decide on what option/s to go with.

The design team must thoroughly evaluate all possibilities of coming up with various product options because one size usually doesn't fit all. Also, as an entrepreneur, you would not just like to serve maximum customers, but would also like to charge more to the customers who have higher purchasing power. The best way to do this is to create suitable product options as a part of the design process.

If the product design team does not come up with product options, the design process should be reworked to ensure that they do consider this. Inability to create options would generally raise questions on the capability of the design team and its process.

## 5. Lack of creativity in pricing

Business models and pricing strategies are not static. Pricing exercise is dynamic. Pricing involves a lot of experimentation and gathering feedback on the results. Moreover, the entrepreneurs must realise that their role doesn't end with demonstrating creativity in coming with a product idea to solve customer's challenges. The customer needs must be satisfied at a price point that is acceptable to the customers.

A fantastic product that resolves customer's problems but fails to do so at a price that the customers afford is a sure recipe for disaster. The entrepreneurs that show creativity is pricing their products for different options and customer segments experience growth in sales and profitability.

The white goods industry's growth has been driven to a considerable extent by partnering with the financiers. The financing option helps customer pay for the product over the long-term, which correlates with the period of usage. Most travel companies have tie-ups with banks and other financiers for financing the travel plans of the customers. That's because most customers don't have enough cash to fund their dreams of travelling to destinations that cost high.

These companies, in partnership with the financiers, provide zero-interest EMI options to ensure that their products are "priced", from the customer's point of view, in line with the customer's affordability.

## 6. Lack of expertise in pricing

E J Bouter, in his book "Pricing: The Third Business Skill – Principles of Price Management", highlights one of the essential distinctive aspects of pricing decisions. There is no one singularly tasked with the responsibility for pricing in an organisation. No one on the board has direct and undivided responsibility for pricing comparable to say, risk management, which is the responsibility of the risk committee of the board, and the Chief Risk Officer (CRO).

"The commercial director is responsible for sales and revenue. The financial director's focus is on accounts and reports, as well as on major financial transactions. The operational director makes sure production is efficient. And the CEO fulfils a coordinating role and is the public face of the company. The pricing policy comes under the competency of the commercial, managing, financial, and operational directors."

As a result of this, most organisations, even large ones, lack expertise in pricing. The pricing is the responsibility of marketing executives who may or may not have sufficient knowledge in pricing. Pricing as a business function is receiving due attention only recently. In the absence of such expertise, organisations depend on the outside experts in taking pricing decisions. Selecting an appropriate expert is critical in such a scenario.

## 7. Challenges of premium positioning

Products and brands that are successfully positioned as premium are legends in the marketing world. The best and the brightest would flock from the business school campuses to work for such companies. Successful premium positioning translates into high visibility and profitability over the long-term. Most would like to associate themselves with such brands and products.

However, positioning the product as a premium product has its unique challenges. Usually, the market for premium products is only a small portion of the entire market for the product. The 'exclusivity' that possessing a premium product conveys is not important enough, and not affordable to most customers, because of preference for functionality over 'brand', and income levels. Building a premium position takes time, and high efforts, and these have to be backed by spending power.

Fundamentally premium positioning is in most cases achieved by identifying a niche and offering a product that delivers best value in that niche. Think of premium brands of watches as an example. Extending this positioning to other products under the same brand is not an easy task. Thus, while premium brands enjoy better pricing and profitability, gaining a larger market share is a challenge for these brands.

Once the premium position is achieved, the brand has to take care that the position is not diluted. When one of the credit cards positioned as an "invitation only" credit card starts mass-mailing "invitation to apply" for the card, the premium positioning is permanently damaged.

## 8. Growth versus profit binary

Ideal business goals of an entrepreneur include high growth in revenues accompanied by high profitability. Growing at a higher rate mostly involves reinvesting back a chunk of profits into initiatives such as brand building, research, development of the intellectual property, technology upgrade, up-skilling human resources, and so on. More than average investment into these futuristic initiatives often means sacrificing profitability and cash flows in the short term.

Thus, most entrepreneurs accept the inevitability of sacrificing one for the other, i.e., trade-off between growth and profitability. The recent increases in private equity funding, where fast-growing start-ups burn cash worth billions of dollars has further re-affirmed the perception that high growth necessarily means low or no profitability and negative cash flows from operations.

One of the ways out of the growth versus profitability binary is to follow a sensible pricing strategy accompanied by a business model that provides scalability at lower fixed costs of operations. While this is not an easy to execute strategy, it is not impossible, given the strong growth and profitability demonstrated by some of the companies like Apple, which has proven to be master of creating product options and pricing them strategically.

## 9. Threat of competition

When your product competes for the customer's wallet share with another, the competition is not likely to sit back and relax. The competitor will also use strategies to position their product better, offer deals that entice the customer in trying their product, and use product options to capture the customer segments that you may not have addressed through your product's options.

Wrong pricing decisions such as fixing an incorrect retail price, wrong channel commissions, wrong estimation of conversion ratios and so on can, therefore, lead to a loss of business to the competitor. If the price change leads to loss of business, the next price changes would be difficult to propose and implement. The experiment once gone wrong sets an example and may reduce the appetite for experimentation, which is an essential part of the process of implementing pricing strategies.

## 10. Culture of freebies

Introductory offers, seasonal sale, festive discounts, clearance sale, event-based pricing and other strategies to attract new customers and sell more to the existing customers often involve giving products for free. Sometime back, most of the food aggregators ran aggressive campaigns to attract new users for their apps. They partnered with the restaurants to sell food at a lower price and in many cases offer some of the dishes like deserts for free if the order size exceeded a certain amount. The app usage saw a massive surge during the initial days. A fair number of customers would have continued higher utilisation of the apps for ordering food at home, due to the habit-forming nature of these innovations.

The culture of offering freebies has become all-pervasive, and customer expectations have been formed accordingly. The sales strategies are designed to offer freebies. Where salespersons are involved in the transaction, they expect the product sales strategies to accommodate the freebies. This is the easy way out for the salesperson to close the sale.

Any attempt at setting prices has to deal with the culture of freebies and the competitor's offers successfully to make a desired impact.

*"Pricing decisions are not easy to make;*
*they are often inherently 'soft'."*

***—William E. Johnson***

# CHAPTER *Fifteen*

## *Executing Pricing Strategy*

*"Dear entrepreneurs: Pricing is branding. Branding is a mindset. Your mindset, not the market, determines how much money you make or don't make. Think about that."*

***—Richie Norton***

Mere knowledge is of no use unless it is put into practice. Having looked at the importance of pricing, its impact on key business goals, various strategies of pricing and the art and science elements involved in the pricing exercise, let's look at how to execute pricing strategy for your business.

## Steps involved in executing pricing strategy

It is difficult to recommend a one-size-fits-all process or methodology for implementing a pricing strategy. The market in which you operate, the stage of business, the phase-in product lifecycle, target customer segment and such factors may need a different approach for each case.

However, most businesses can design their execution strategy using the below mentioned 10 steps as their baseline.

1. Evaluate pricing strategies used in your industry
2. Evaluate strategies relevant to your product or service

3. Review the current strategy and analyse gaps
4. Review product design capabilities and process
5. Review business goals and alignment with pricing strategy
6. Create a plan to fill the gaps in pricing strategy
7. The model financial impact of changes in pricing
8. Assign responsibilities and develop pricing expertise
9. Experiment with pricing and gather feedback
10. Develop a culture that values pricing capability

Each of these steps is explained below.

## 1. Evaluate pricing strategies used in your industry

Understanding the pricing strategies used by the other players is a good start to evaluate the strategies that you may want to use, besides the added benefit of understanding what the competitors are doing to win business.

Pricing strategies used by commodities manufacturers, e.g., steel and cement, could be different from other industries like fast-moving consumer durables (FMCG), shipping, insurance, technology, and so on. Moreover, within the same industry, those who execute projects may follow different strategies when compared to those selling products or providing services.

Within the same industry, e.g., food and beverages, those selling packaged food will use a different strategy from those selling ready-to-eat packaged food, caterers, restaurants, quick-service restaurant chains and those who run business in franchise mode. The business-to-business pricing strategy in the food industry would be different from the company to consumer pricing strategy.

Additionally, the level of technology usage, innovation, dynamism, risk-taking capability, location and business model influence the pricing strategy.

Analysing the local, regional, national and international pricing strategies used in the industry can provide a lot of insights that can be used locally. Changing demand and supply scenarios, vagaries of seasonality and business cycles offer additional opportunities to study. Moreover, there is always an opportunity for cross-industry learnings that can be implemented in your industry.

A focused pricing team should continuously develop a database of ideas from their study and evaluate those for suitability in their business.

## 2. Evaluate strategies relevant to your product or service

Number of factors impact the evaluation of pricing strategies in the context of your products or services. Some of these factors include

a. Business model - the flexibility in making changes, such as outright purchase versus outsourced manufacturing versus in-house manufacturing, distribution network etc.

b. Composition of key elements of cost – fixed costs, semi-variable costs and variable costs
c. The ticket size of the typical deal – the outlay and decision-making process from customer's point of view
d. Frequency of purchase of the product by the customer – frequent purchase, periodic purchased or rare/one-time purchase
e. Nature of the product - tangible or intangible, and the impact on the ease of purchase, cost of delivery and subsequent support
f. Price elasticity of demand - measure of the relationship between a change in the quantity demanded and the difference in its price.
g. Customer need satisfied – whether the product is classified as essential, comfort or luxury by the customer
h. Regulation around the product – on product manufacturing, distribution, sale and pricing

Moreover, the pricing strategy is also influenced by whether the product benefits are delivered by undertaking a customer specific project, and how much the service element in delivery is critical for customer satisfaction.

## 3. Review the current strategy and analyse gaps

Assessment of the current pricing strategy is a prerequisite to improvement. The questionnaire in chapter 04 – "Assess your current pricing strategy" would be a high starting point in assessing the current strategy. Most businesses that are in existence for a few years are found to score between 50 to 60 on an honest assessment of their existing strategy.

The assessment reflects contribution of the marketing, sales and finance teams in developing a sound pricing strategy. The areas evaluated include

1. Identification of customer segments
2. Choice of marketing and sales channels
3. Cost of customer acquisition
4. Quantifying customer value delivered
5. Forecasted Cash flows and budgets
6. Offering risk- reward-based solution
7. Deep understanding of product benefits
8. Product and solution variants
9. Resolving customer buying objections
10. Demonstrating confidence in the product

You can access a more detailed questionnaire for assessing your pricing strategy at www.cfoaxis.com.

## 4. Review product design capabilities and process

In general, the goal of product design is to build a product or a service that meets the customer need by delivering the functionality within the agreed time and cost. Additionally, as discussed earlier, the product design team should come up with the product variants that meet the needs of different customers at the price that they would like to pay for. This is essential to differentiate vis-à-vis the competition, set an 'anchor', increase conversions, increase revenue and enhance profitability.

The product design team must, therefore, have the necessary skills to deliver on this expectation. The critical skills needed in the team include surveying, requirements gathering, problem-solving, design thinking, design specification, user experience (UX) and user interface (UI), modelling and prototyping, computer-aided design, quality standards and specifications, creativity and imagination and engineering, besides generic skills such as communication, information technology, teamwork and leadership.

Additionally, the product design team should have the following skills which overlap with the other teams: market research, data analytics, business and commercial acumen, and regulatory compliance.

The product design team, along with marketing teams, should provide inputs to the finance team for data analysis, financial analysis, costing and financial modelling.

The product design team's capabilities should be evaluated in this context. If needed, investments should be made to train the team in additional skills, or hire new team members, o=r engage vendors who provide those skills.

## 5. Review business goals and alignment with pricing strategy

In "chapter 2: price = growth + profitability", we looked at how change in prices has a significant impact on growth and profitability.

Businesses that want to grow fast in terms of sales, customers and markets will develop a product portfolio that appeals to a broader customer base. They will most likely invest in building multiple brands that position them across the spectrum, right from premium to mass market. The pricing will be set to deliver optimum target profitability across different products and variants.

Businesses that focus on profitability through positioning will focus on a niche and grow through premium positioning. The niche itself can be expanded by offering more products within the niche, e.g., within 2- wheeler segment. The overall market share may be sacrificed for profits.

If dominating the market through large market share is the target, the business may price products such that the growth is very fast as compared to the competitors. This may call for running losses and large cash burn.

It is, therefore, crucial that the alignment between the pricing strategy and the critical business goals is carefully examined for course correction and ensuring the synchronisation.

## 6. Create a plan to fill the gaps in pricing strategy

Having analysed the disparities in pricing strategy using the questionnaire, review of the product design capabilities and process and re-examination of alignment between business goals and pricing strategy, the gaps must be filled. This, however, may not be a short, one-time and straight forward task. Hence a clear plan with goals, tasks, owner/s and timelines should be drawn up, to ensure that

1. The customer segments and marketing and sales channels are re-aligned
2. The lifetime value of the customer is in line with the cost of customer acquisition and the customer value delivered
3. Product design capabilities are enhanced with suitable skills, budget and freedom to work within the matrix reporting structure
4. A comprehensive re-evaluation of the product benefits is undertaken by involving customers and product, and solution variants are created

5. Relevant pricing strategies are identified for leveraging innovation and creativity and embedding risk-reward elements
6. The sales team is re-trained to handle customer buying objections and demonstrate confidence in the product
7. Appropriate financial models are built and tested for forecasting and back-testing impact on growth, profitability and cash flows

Since pricing strategy keeps evolving, necessary feedback and review should be built-in so that the CEO, as an executive facing the board, is armed with the essential information to get buy-in.

## 7. The model financial impact of changes in pricing

Changes in prices have a direct effect on customer segments, target market, conversions, revenue, customer lifetime value, cost of customer acquisition and profitability. It is, therefore, that the business develops a financial model that helps simulate the likely impact of change in pricing strategy on these critical business performance indicators. The forecast created from these changes is also vital for providing the visibility of projected financial performance to the investors.

A comprehensive financial model would include the products, services, the product and services variants, their prices, the customer segments and target population, expected conversions, sales and marketing costs, cost of customer acquisition, and lifetime value of the customer, and the resultant impact of these on profitability, cash flows and business valuation.

*"When compared to cutting costs, increasing sales, or spending more on advertising and publicity, raising prices is a more powerful profit lever."*

***—Utpal Dholakia***

The financial model should also provide visibility on the product profitability, portfolio profitability, geography wise profitability, channel-wise profitability and such other relevant performance indicators, and support decision-making, e.g., decisions regarding prices, commissions to distributors, online marketers, franchise owners etc. The impact on the other price-related factors such as the discounts, special offers, guarantees and warranties, maintenance and support contracts also should be visible.

The model should be tested by comparing with the actual results and should continuously evolve based on the experience over some time.

## 8. Assign responsibilities and develop pricing expertise

Over the years, several businesses have realised that pricing strategy is vital to the long-term success of the business. However, pricing requires multidisciplinary skills, that cut across traditional strategy, marketing, sales, finance and other domains.

You would not find pricing responsibility allocated to someone on the board of directors of the company, unlike risk management, auditing, and management compensation and succession planning, which is often assigned to a committee of the board. Therefore, developing pricing expertise needs answer to a question, as to who will ultimately own the responsibility for developing that expertise within the organisation. Most organisations are likely to place this responsibility on the CMO or the CFO.

The responsibility should be fixed clearly, and the decisions are not left to lower levels. The pricing team should have clarity of the roles, and the key performance indicators and the incentives should be well defined. The guidelines that govern the price-setting exercise should be clear. In case the external expertise is obtained, the consultants should be identified and remunerated accordingly.

## 9. Experiment with pricing and gather feedback

Formulating a pricing strategy is very important for startups before they crystalise their business plan. The business which is running for some time can also benefit from taking a fresh perspective on their pricing strategy because price once set, is not carved in stone. There will be some resistance from the customers and the salespersons if they perceive that the change in prices is not favourable to them. Therefore, communication of change, as well as planning the rollout is critical.

> *"What I 'charge' today has nothing to do with yesterday or tomorrow. It has to do with 'now'!"*
>
> ***—David Wayne Wilson***
>
> *[Pricing News Daily, 2014]*

Once the decision on pricing is taken, the marketing team should re-align the branding, positioning and promotion activities accordingly. The branding and positioning are difficult to change; hence a shift in positioning may require that the products are launched under a different brand altogether. Communicating the price to the customer is not enough; the clarity on pricing strategy should exist within the sales team, channel partners and finance and operations teams as well. The sales team should be able to articulate the return on investment to the customers in line with the price. The finance team should be able to test the back-test the price for appropriateness using past data.

The change in pricing can experiment in a specific product version, a channel, a location, or a geography. In some cases, special offers can be launched to check the customer response to the changed prices. Customer surveys can provide additional feedback, besides the sales metrics after the launch with new prices. Pricing is a continuous exercise, and pricing team should be engaged in monitoring the impact and making changes as appropriate.

## 10. Develop a culture that values pricing capability

While the responsibility for pricing can be fixed with a CMO or a CFO, the change in pricing strategy would need a difference in the organisation culture. In general, the culture of the organisation has to move from focusing cost to focusing on price and revenue. Everyone in the organisation should know the company's pricing philosophy.

The change in mindset is critical, especially for the marketing and sales teams. The marketing teams have to craft competitive tactics and messaging in line with the pricing strategy. The sales teams will have to be convinced that the new strategy will increase sales and protect or enhance their commissions. The sales team may have to be re-trained from time to time to bolster their confidence, and the sales playbook should be updated to help them make decisions to strike the deal, and handle customer objections.

The responsibility for the change in culture is, therefore, squarely with the CEO. The CEO must drive the move and not leave it to the CMO or CFO, who is in charge of the pricing strategy. The board should make this cultural shift as a critical criterion for measuring CEOs performance.

## Leading the execution of pricing strategy

The pricing strategy formulation and implementation requires a multidisciplinary approach. The following table shows recommended leadership and support roles that the different leaders may be assigned for the various stage of implementation. Each organisation should devise its mechanism.

| *Step in executing the pricing strategy* | *CEO* | *CMO* | *CSO* | *CFO* |
|---|---|---|---|---|
| Evaluate pricing strategies used in your industry | Support | Lead | Support | Support |
| Evaluate strategies relevant to your product/ service | Support | Lead | Support | Support |
| Review the current strategy and analyse gaps | Support | Lead | Support | Lead |
| Review product design capabilities and process | Support | Lead | Support | Support |
| Review business goals and alignment with pricing strategy | Lead | Support | Support | Lead |
| Create a plan to fill the gaps in pricing strategy | Lead | Support | Support | Support |
| The model financial impact of changes in pricing | Support | Support | Support | Lead |
| Assign responsibilities and develop pricing expertise | Lead | Support | Support | Support |
| Experiment with pricing and gather feedback | Support | Support | Lead | Support |
| Develop a culture that values pricing capability | Lead | Support | Support | Support |

Looking at the complexity, a separate cross-functional team under CMO or CFO, with a dotted line of reporting to the other CXOs could be tasked with handling this exercise.

> *"Do not compromise on the quality and*
> *your customers will not negotiate on the price."*
>
> ***—Amit Kalantri***

# *References*

## Books

Pricing: The Third Business Skill- Principles of rice Management, by E J Bouter

Thinking, fast and slow, by Daniel Kahneman

Predictably Irrational – The hidden forces that shape our decisions, by Dan Ariely

How to Price Effectively, by Utpal Dholakia

Priced to Influence, by Utpal Dholakia

Pricing – how to price your product, by Gary Beeson

The Win without pitching manifesto, by Blair Enns

www.ingramcontent.com/pod-product-compliance
Lightning Source LLC
LaVergne TN
LVHW041152150826
845673LV00001B/138

* 9 7 8 9 3 8 9 0 2 4 6 1 6 *